OVERCOMING
BARRIERS TO LEARNING

After initially training and working as a nurse, then as a Health Visitor and completing a degree with the Open University, **Sheila Mulvenney** first started to teach mature students on Child Care and Care Management courses at undergraduate, HNC/D or National Diploma level. She became aware that many mature students still had obstacles to overcome from their background or previous learning experiences, and a number struggled with literacy. It has been very pleasing for her to work with social workers who had completed their initial training on courses she managed and delivered.

After completing a PGCE, Sheila went on to work in a number of different settings with younger students, often with those who experienced social, emotional or behavioural difficulties, had other special educational needs or were looked after. Her roles included being a SENCo in a specialist provision and Head Teacher of a small school for students who were all in care and resident within the organisation.

These roles led to work in local authorities focussing on behaviour or inclusion and then with children in care as Head of a Virtual School. In addition, Sheila is a qualified Sounds-Write trainer, regularly running phonics courses for teachers in schools. She is also qualified as a teacher of English as a foreign language, having taught English to, and hosted, a large number of students from other countries.

Her interest in meeting the emotional needs of children in care led her to train as a therapist in Emotional Freedom Techniques, and she now runs her own company offering training, tuition, therapy and consultancy to individuals, schools and other organisations and undertakes various interim appointments within local authorities.

OVERCOMING BARRIERS TO LEARNING

How a culture of care in schools helps troubled pupils learn

Sheila Mulvenney

Worth Publishing

worthpublishing.com

First published 2017 by Worth Publishing Ltd

worthpublishing.com

Printed and bound in Great Britain by TJ International, Padstow, Cornwall

British Library Cataloguing in Publication Data
A catalogue record for this book is available from the British Library

ISBN 9781903269275

Cover and text design by Anna Murphy
Front cover image ©Image Source

To the tireless supporters who are my husband and family,
whose warmth, love and humour provides inspiration every day - and to my parents,
who ensured as I grew up that I went to sleep every night feeling loved.

ATTACHMENT AWARE SCHOOLS COLLECTION®

The Attachment Aware School series

Book 1   The Key Adult in School
Book 2   The Senior Manager in School
Book 3   The Key Teacher in School
Book 4   The Team Pupil in School
Book 5   The Parent and Carer in School

Attachment for Teachers
Attachment in the Classroom
Better Play
Conversations That Matter
Inside I'm Hurting
Little-Mouse Finds a Safe Place
Overcoming Barriers to Learning
School as a Secure Base
Settling to Learn
Teaching the Unteachable
Teenagers and Attachment
Temper Temper!
What About Me?
What Can I Do With The Kid Who...?
You think I'm Evil

Acknowledgements

The content of this book is the result of my own learning journey, having worked in a variety of care and education settings starting in hospitals, moving to the community and then into schools and other contexts before working in various capacities for local authorities. This has brought me into contact with many children and adults who have experienced all manner of challenges and difficulties, and with those working tirelessly and expertly with these traumatised or distressed individuals. I cannot begin to measure what I have learned from these people. Sadly I also have come across a number of professionals who, for a variety of reasons both personal and professional, 'got it wrong': but honest reflection sometimes still allowed for learning.

I would particularly like to thank the following groups and individuals.

- *Teachers:* I have been privileged to witness not only excellent teaching, but sensitive, innovative and creative caring responses to children and young people who are clearly 'troubled'. The way some teachers have been able to build relationships with and engage some of the hardest to engage students has truly been an inspiration.

- *Teaching Assistants, learning mentors and pastoral staff:* I am grateful to many of the other staff within schools, sometimes working with little support, training or experience, with some of the most troubled children and young people. The impact of the individuals who manage amidst the challenges to show care and compassion day after day has been humbling and taught me a lot about the power of supportive relationships for children who have or are experiencing stress or trauma.

- *Social workers:* I have been privileged to work with some social workers who manage to demonstrate, amidst increasing organisational pressures, and constantly under fire from press and public, a determination to always act in the best interests of the child and to advocate tirelessly on their behalf. Though not always comfortable, I have learned so much from some of the often contentious conversations we have shared and the difficult decisions that have needed to be made.

- *Other professionals:* From educational psychologists and behaviour support teachers to legal teams, IRO's and managers at every level and in numerous areas throughout the country, I have learned that different perspectives can create a fuller picture and when facing challenges, candid conversations can help to support and challenge and hopefully improve the service provided to some of the most vulnerable in society.

- *Carers:* Individual carers vary in the strengths and qualities they have and the level of support they can offer to children and young people. I am fortunate to have met, worked with and learned from some that have shown not only dedication, commitment and excellence in day to day care, but insight and expertise in managing and nurturing some very distressed and traumatised children and young people.

- *Children and young people*: It is a privilege to have worked with a large number of children either in care, or experiencing other social or emotional 'challenges'. I have been amazed at the resilience they can show in times of real struggle, at their determination at times to be 'children', at their ability to accept the imperfections and inconsistencies of the adults and organisations and at their ability at times to enjoy 'moments' and to appreciate and show humour. I am confident that I will continue to learn from the children and young people with whom I come into contact and on whose behalf I work.

I would also like to thank Andrea Perry of Worth Publishing. Without her expertise there would be no book and she has managed to aptly demonstrate how essential both support and challenge are in any learning process.

Contents

Introduction Making a difference

Working in a wide variety of educational settings over several decades I have often been aware of the children and young people in the class who find it hard to access the curriculum. Sometimes this is because of a special educational need, or a difficulty with reading, for example. But on other occasions it's become obvious that the obstacles to learning they face are of a social or emotional nature.

While children in the care of local authorities may represent only a half of one per cent of the school population, we are all aware that there are a much greater number of pupils and students in our classrooms who are struggling with a whole range of social and emotional problems, and perhaps experiencing milder forms of violence, abuse or neglect. There may also be those who have difficulty forming relationships because they have never experienced any meaningful attachments with adults able to meet their needs for security and safety. Others may be experiencing parental break-ups or live in families struggling with illness, disability, trauma, addictions, dependencies or severe financial difficulties. There may be bereavement in the family, or separation through postings overseas, imprisonment or countless other reasons. Affected day to day by these different factors at home, across what I'll be describing as the 'spectrum of trouble', these children and young people are in our classrooms, but they may well be unable to learn.

I remain amazed at the resilience that some of these pupils and students demonstrate in the face of what can be extreme difficulties and trauma. But sometimes, unsurprisingly, they simply can't concentrate on 'work': they can't always manage their emotions appropriately and they don't always behave in the way we would expect or want as the adults who work with them in our schools and educational settings.

Sometimes a pupil who is disruptive must be removed from a classroom setting in order for others to learn. This is completely understandable, indeed, sometimes essential. But unless something happens to address the needs of the vulnerable student when they are out of the classroom, the likelihood is that the situation will be repeated, and over time, the difficulties that caused the student to be removed in the first place are likely to get worse. That 'something' will only happen if the school culture supports it.

We adults also experience the whole range of emotions. We react and respond to all the diverse stimuli that living in a modern world brings, coping with the traumas, minor or major, that happen throughout our own lives. Our choice to work in education also means that alongside teaching the curriculum, we need to manage the additional demands of working with our troubled students. Regrettably, many staff don't feel supported to do so, as if this were an incidental aspect of the job or simply something to manage away with zero tolerance behaviourist policies. Coping with the ever multiplying demands of the job and the conflict of trying to meet students' diverse needs and ensure high quality teaching and learning takes place, whilst some students struggle and may also be stopping others learning, can leave staff feeling frustrated, exhausted and alone.

My understanding is that in the current political, social and economic environment there is likely to be an increase in the number of children and young people within our schools who could be described as troubled and vulnerable, and who will definitely not be in a place where they are consistently ready to learn. In addition, the changes within education, which over recent years seem to have been unprecedented in scope and number, have squeezed schools in terms of the time needed to deliver an ever-changing curriculum with new assessment protocols and an increasing focus on academic outcomes with little regard it seems for other 'results'.

In some places this combination of factors has led to an overworked and demoralised staff - I rarely visit a school where staff seem relaxed or have time to attend meetings without substantial juggling of their responsibilities. I see them check their watches, and their phones, and I know that many of my emails are likely to be answered by school staff at 10pm. I am also aware of staff who, every day, go the extra mile to support those struggling learners, thinking of new approaches and strategies that might be effective in helping their students learn. But this isn't a sustainable work pattern, especially when the emotional drain of working with troubled or vulnerable young people must also be considered.

Creating a caring culture in every school, where all staff feel valued and supported will enable us, as the adults, to offer the care and support these vulnerable students need. Developing an understanding of the trauma that many of the students experience, the appeals for help and support they may be communicating through their often disruptive or even abusive behaviour, and having strategies to support these vulnerable learners, will create a team of professionals who are better equipped to meet the challenges such students present. It will also be a culture that supports all the adults who are giving of themselves each and every day to develop the much needed relationships with those who are not yet in a place where they can learn. My hope is that through reading this book and completing the reflective activities, you will be more aware not only of the needs of your students but of your own needs, and the way you deal with your own thoughts and emotions to preserve and enhance your resilience.

I often hear in schools and meetings about students who have experienced 'trouble' of some kind that what they need is firm boundaries and consistency. That's obviously true: at some level we all need these to feel safe and secure. But our pupils also need compassion. When you are hurt and vulnerable, when life has delivered knock after knock, kindness and compassion can go a long way. It needs to be a constructive compassion, not a *"There, there,"* approach, but rather a consistent, deliberate, well-informed attempt to form relationships of trust and respect so that these hurt and vulnerable children and young people can feel our acceptance and empathy, and then go on to learn different ways of coping with the impact of the trauma and trouble they have experienced.

Schools are designed to be places of learning. What learning actually means can be wide-ranging: the skills many of the vulnerable children and young people need to learn can be accessed best through care and nurturing relationships. They may first need to learn about themselves and their emotions, and about relationships and social skills, before they will be in a place where they can learn what we may regard as academic skills. Sometimes adults in schools worry that they may not be the best person to offer this type of help. But so often we are the person who is on hand, perhaps the person the student has a relationship with. So if for whatever reason we can't or don't offer the help the child or young person needs, their struggle is likely to continue, or worsen … until some help is offered.

As humans who work with people, I would suggest we as a profession are on the whole, compassionate, kind and hardworking. We want to see children grow and develop in all areas of their life at a pace which they can manage. In my experience we are prepared to give substantially of our own resources in terms of time, effort and our own emotions to achieve this. My hope is simply that this book will help in that process, equipping adults to nurture and support these pupils and students until they are in place where they are able to learn. You'll find alternative strategies for working with students who aren't yet able to learn or even indeed function effectively in the social and emotional environment of a school. And I hope that you'll feel a renewed sense of enthusiasm and optimism for this all-important work, and a greater belief in your own capacity to contribute and make a difference.

CHAPTER 1

Being ready to learn

Introduction

I will begin this chapter by looking at the process of learning, recognising it as a natural, automatic process for young children when provided with the right learning opportunities. Then we'll think about how learning and development in young children follow a particular sequence, and look at the differing ways in which individuals learn best. I'll also highlight styles and motivations for learning before looking at the context and situations that can help or prevent a child or young person being ready to learn.

Programmed to learn

Learning is natural. Watch a small child playing and you'll be left in no doubt. Look at a small child playing with water; notice how she watches it pour, filling pots of different sizes, continuing to pour while the water overflows, tipping it from one container to another, letting it spill, touching it, tasting it and then repeating everything all over again. There may not be anything concrete to show for it, apart from a wet floor and probably a wet child; but I think most of us would agree that learning will be taking place.

Young children also show great determination. A toddler falls over countless times when he's learning to walk but is generally happy to keep getting up and trying again. Young children may become frustrated with difficult tasks, but most toddlers are happy to keep practising emerging skills repeatedly, especially with encouragement, and with most skills their perseverance pays off and they are successful in the end.

We're all individuals, and while our learning processes may be different we all have brains which work in fundamentally similar ways. The right opportunities need to be presented if learning is to take place. So as a very simple example, a baby who is never put on the floor will find it hard to learn to crawl. An older child who has never used scissors before will find it hard to cut out even a simple shape and a teenager who has never had access to a bicycle would not be able to get on and instantly ride. Learning is natural, but we need the right situation or environment for it to take place, and different individuals may have different ways in which they learn most effectively (often known as 'learning styles').

Learning styles

It's long been recognised that there are different learning styles and while we can all learn in different ways, some styles and types of learning suit some individuals better than others. Many factors influence an individual's learning style; genetic makeup, personality, previous experience and culture all play a part. Learning styles have been categorised in different ways: one commonly used approach is that of Bandler & Grinder (1975) who identify visual, auditory, kinaesthetic, and tactile as being four 'styles' of learning. McCarthy (2005) classified different individuals as being innovative, analytical, dynamic or common sense learners. Most teachers would acknowledge that they endeavour to offer a range of different learning activities to hopefully give all learners a chance to have some material in a style that suits their learning. Presenting varied material in a range of different styles will have the greatest chance of sustaining interest within the whole group.

More recently however, it has been suggested (Lilienfield et al 2009) that while it may be useful to present information in a way which suits an individual's preferred learning style it is also important to 'challenge' ourselves and our learners by providing exposure to material in a variety of styles. It's important to remember that here we are talking about *the way* material is presented, rather than the material itself. If you want to teach about the five senses, for example, you could provide a worksheet (visual), watch a DVD presentation (auditory and visual), and/or get children experiencing their senses by perhaps moving through different stations in the classroom (kinaesthetic) where they use their senses by seeing, hearing, smelling, tasting and touching (tactile). What is actually presented, in any of these ways, is the curriculum.

Curriculum

The curriculum is the actual information presented to children or young people and the skills that are explicitly taught. In most state schools this is all defined in considerable detail for each key stage: many teachers would probably say that currently there is little flexibility within this, given the parallel frameworks of assessment and inspections. It is also subject to frequent change. This is not the place to consider the curriculum in detail, but I'll look at the different areas of it in the foundation stage as this can help us understand the kind of progress that's expected when learning is taking place effectively. It illuminates some of the general principles about learning and development that I'll be exploring below, and the impact that this early learning may have on later readiness to learn.

The Early Years Foundation Stage curriculum identifies different areas of learning known as Early Learning Goals, and while progress in all areas is desirable, it is possible for children to make global progress, generally moving forward, while progressing at a faster pace in some areas and at a slower pace in others. Development is sequential: most toddlers utter sounds and single words before sentences and they usually sit upright before they stand. But development can also happen in a step-like fashion where immense progress is made over a short time followed by a plateau with regard to learning in that area.

The statutory framework for the Early Year's Foundation Stage (2014) stresses the need to 'ignite children's curiosity and enthusiasm for learning' and identified seven areas of learning.

1. COMMUNICATION AND
   LANGUAGE
2. PHYSICAL DEVELOPMENT
3. PERSONAL, SOCIAL AND
   EMOTIONAL DEVELOPMENT

4. LITERACY
5. MATHEMATICS
6. UNDERSTANDING THE WORLD
7. EXPRESSIVE ART AND DESIGN

The first three areas are seen as the prime areas of learning. It's widely recognised that if there are any problems with these, then development in the other four areas may also be adversely affected. For example, a child who finds verbal communication difficult may find the progression to literacy very hard: or a child who has a physical difficulty, for example problems with fine motor skills, may have problems holding a pencil or paintbrush and taking part in expressive art. Children who have issues in the area of personal, social and emotional development may have difficulties with peers, may have difficulty sitting still, may find any interaction with others a challenge, and may find the less structured parts of the day hard to enjoy. Mealtimes may be an issue, and they may need support with going to the toilet or following any sort of instruction.

In many ways then, these first three key areas are the foundation stones of learning. Some children may have a specific problem with literacy or mathematics, but children who have problems with any or all of the three prime areas are likely to need considerable support if progress is to be made in other areas. As children progress through the education system, growing in size and developing complex skills, there will be some who still struggle to achieve the progress that would be expected in the three key areas. Each is subdivided into goals - these are listed opposite, and children are expected to achieve these in the Early Years Foundation Stage.

As you read them through, think about some of the pupils and students you work with - how many are still struggling with these prime areas?

The statutory framework for the Early Year's Foundation Stage can be accessed at education.gov.uk/schools/teachingandlearning/curriculum/a0068102/early-years-foundation-stage-eyfs

1. COMMUNICATION AND LANGUAGE	2. PHYSICAL DEVELOPMENT	3. PERSONAL SOCIAL AND EMOTIONAL DEVELOPMENT
LISTENING AND ATTENTION *Children listen attentively in a range of situations.* *They listen to stories, accurately anticipating key events and respond to what they hear with relevant comments, questions or actions.* *They give their attention to what others say and respond appropriately, while engaged in another activity.*	**MOVING AND HANDLING** *Children show good control and co-ordination in large and small movements.* *They move confidently in a range of ways, safely negotiating space.* *They handle equipment and tools effectively, including pencils for writing.*	**SELF-CONFIDENCE AND SELF-AWARENESS** *Children are confident to try new activities, and say why they like some activities more than others.* *They are confident to speak in a familiar group, will talk about their ideas, and will choose the resources they need for their activities.* *They say when they do or don't need help.*
UNDERSTANDING *Children follow instructions involving several ideas or actions.* *They answer 'how' and 'why' questions about their experiences and in response to stories or events.*	**HEALTH AND SELF-CARE** *Children know the importance for good health of physical exercise, and a healthy diet, and talk about ways to keep healthy and safe.* *They manage their own basic hygiene and personal needs successfully, including dressing and going to the toilet independently.*	**MANAGING FEELINGS AND BEHAVIOUR** *Children talk about how they and others show feelings, talk about their own and others' behaviour, and its consequences, and know that some behaviour is unacceptable.* *They work as part of a group or class, and understand and follow the rules.* *They adjust their behaviour to different situations, and take changes of routine in their stride.*
SPEAKING *Children express themselves effectively, showing awareness of listeners' needs.* *They use past, present and future forms accurately when talking about events that have happened or are to happen in the future.* *They develop their own narratives and explanations by connecting ideas or events.*		**MAKING RELATIONSHIPS** *Children play co-operatively, taking turns with others.* *They take account of one another's ideas about how to organise their activity.* *They show sensitivity to others' needs and feelings, and form positive relationships with adults and other children.*

Dean was 13 when I met him and had been permanently excluded from a mainstream school. He was fairly average in terms of size and physical development. He was also a fluent reader and was able to complete many maths tasks well, though accurate assessment was made difficult by the problems he had in maintaining attention or even staying in one place for the time required. Dean had many problems with peers and they would often complain that he sat or stood far too close to them. Dean would talk very loudly and shout out frequently in lessons: he would become angry easily and 'storm out' of the classroom at the smallest provocation.

Some areas of development had happened smoothly for Dean, but undoubtedly others had not, for whatever reason. The problem was made worse by the fact that we all expected Dean to behave in the way other 13 year olds did, but Dean simply hadn't developed the necessary skills he needed to do that. As he had grown chronologically older, he had moved to school settings that no longer offered support for many of the areas of learning with which he struggled. He was increasingly expected to cope with change, communicate effectively, manage his physical movement and 'space' and would be told off or sanctioned for not managing this effectively when actually he probably just did not have the skills.

The curriculum is set nationally, but the way each child progresses through it and the pace at which they do so is different for every pupil. As we'll continue to see in the next section, there's a relationship between the different areas of learning. If there is a problem in one area, this may have an impact on the learning that can take place in others.

Areas of learning

It's clear that a relationship exists between the different areas of learning, while each area can also be seen as distinct in terms of assessment. A pupil who lacks confidence in his physical skills may find it more difficult to enjoy sports or games which require physical prowess. If he isn't supported, this lack of confidence is likely to impact further on his social development as he may 'avoid playtimes' when physical activity is expected.

Research from the Institute of Fiscal studies reported by the BBC in 2011 showed that the seven year olds born in August were 2.5 to 3.5 times more likely to be regarded by their teachers as 'below average' in reading, writing and maths than those born in September. Having 'fixed' statutory school 'years' means that in any one year there could be a 12 month gap between the youngest and the oldest and when children are four or five, or even seven or eight, this can show itself markedly in the development and maturity of the children. There was also an increased likelihood of August born children being unhappy at school and experiencing bullying. Indeed the gap still seems to exist by the end of secondary school, as this cohort is 20% less likely to attend a leading university and in fact may end up doing worse throughout their working life than their September born peers.

If you were in a class as a child, and some of you will have been, with children who were almost a year older, physically bigger and stronger and possibly more able in many other areas of development than you, and if each day you struggled to achieve what they seemed to do with ease - might this have had an impact on the way you saw yourself and your ability to learn in relation to others? The likelihood is that it would, and this is borne out by the statistics.

In addition, many school staff have recognised that this pattern seems especially true for boys. In a society like ours, which still values physical strength and aptitude in males, if young boys find sport difficult at first they may shy away from it. The same may well be true for academic skills, as research shows that there are key differences in the way boys and girls behave in classroom settings. Boys for example tend to overestimate their academic abilities whereas girls tend to underestimate theirs, and therefore have a tendency to work harder (Cole et al 2009)

The research simply demonstrates that development follows a chronological sequence, but that in any given cohort of children there will be numerous variations because of age, gender, environmental experience, family, genetic predisposition and possibly, pathology, by which I mean those children who because of illness or disability have particular difficulties with aspects of learning.

There are distinct areas of learning that can be used to assess progress and provide a structure for the curriculum. But children will always learn as individuals within this framework. They are not only learning the curriculum offer, they are learning about themselves, gaining impressions of what they can and can't do well, constantly either consciously or sub-consciously adjusting their behaviour to ensure their needs are met as they respond to others in the environment. Children and young people don't just learn in lessons from teachers, they spend their whole day learning - though it may not always be the kind of learning that we as their teachers, school staff or parents, would hope is taking place!

We have probably all encountered pupils and students who learn everything from swear words to drug habits from their peers, and those who adopt the behaviours they have seen their peers exhibiting if they can see there are some gains. We are also all aware that adult attention, even negative adult attention, will be seen by many children as a gain. The adult-child ratios prescribed for school and nursery settings suggest that as a child gets older the need for individual adult attention should diminish. But although the child may be chronologically older, their individual level of personal, social and emotional development may mean that their demand for attention is a lot higher than might be expected for the average child of their age. This will have implications for the way they learn, and the support they may need in order to learn, and for the relationships they develop with both their peers and the adults around them.

Formal and informal learning

As school staff we may concentrate on formal learning opportunities, but we are aware that learning can occur at any point during the day: in lessons, at playtime or break time, on the way to school, in the corridor, or eating lunch, to mention just a few. The case study below shows that learning can happen informally, that children learn from each other, and that while this may happen at any time it can be encouraged when a framework is given.

Caitlin attended a school that had a rich ethnic diversity and a fairly transient population. When she was five years old she went home with a certificate for being very welcoming to a new student. Her parents asked about it, and she told them about Oleksim, who had just arrived from Poland and spoke no English. She told them brightly how she wanted to be friendly but wasn't sure what to do, as he wouldn't understand 'Hello'. Her parents asked what she did and she said that she smiled, pointed at the climbing frame and nodded her head and they both went and played on it for the rest of the playtime and then again at lunchtime. When her parents mentioned this to the class teacher the following morning, the teacher said she had been particularly glad as she had asked the whole class to think about ways they could be friendly and welcoming to Oleksim. Hopefully this was a positive learning experience for Oleksim as well as Caitlin.

Undoubtedly the teacher had provided the framework for learning but much of the learning occurred during the playtime. In this case it was a positive experience for all, and that's the kind we would hope children are gathering: but informal learning may not always be positive. As parents, teachers and probably as adults who were once children, we will all have examples of learning that were negative: being laughed at by our classmates because of something we said or wore, or being in the dreaded last place when the team captains 'chose' the teams. It's now recognised that experiences like these can be detrimental for the emotional and sometimes physical wellbeing of a child. Such incidents may now be recognised as bullying, with schools and other organisations working hard not only to raise awareness but to provide preventative strategies and resolution frameworks. The NSPCC (2016) reported that there were almost 26,000 counselling sessions with children about bullying in that year, and bullying was the biggest reason children under 11 contacted ChildLine.

Informal learning is really important. Our pupils can learn to make and keep friends, enjoy laughing with others in a solidarity within which they share, resolve conflict, and experience and often learn to 'manage' a whole range of emotions. But whether or not these experiences are positive will depend on the structures that are in place to protect the children and young people who may be vulnerable for a variety of reasons in situations of informal learning. In the 2015 annual bullying survey by the charity *Ditch the Label*, 43% of young people aged 13-20 reported being bullied and 69% reported witnessing bullying. Of course bullying may occur in classrooms, but there are far more opportunities at times when the adult to child/young person ratio is lower and the physical area much larger, such as at breaks and playtimes (*and see* p.24).

Children will learn from the situations they experience and from the people around them. This kind of learning is often in the area of personal, social and emotional learning. Our hope would always be that these learning situations are positive, but sadly for many children and young people they aren't. We wouldn't dream of letting a five year old play unsupervised with groups of teenagers without putting certain safeguards in place, yet every day we release onto the playground socially and emotionally immature children with minimal supervision, and what they learn about themselves and the world around them at those times will have an impact on what they are able and ready to learn back in class.

When it comes to formal learning within the classroom, of course there are optimal situations in terms of class size and the environment for example, and naturally the state of readiness to learn of the individual pupils or young people will be crucial.

Maslow's hierarchy of needs

While learning can happen anywhere and at any time, formal learning is usually most effective when individuals have their basic needs met. As humans, we are better able to function and learn when we are not too cold, too hungry or too tired. We need to feel safe and have a sense of belonging through having some kind of secure relationship. The diagram below shows what Malsow called the 'Hierarchy of Needs' (Maslow, 1943, 2013).

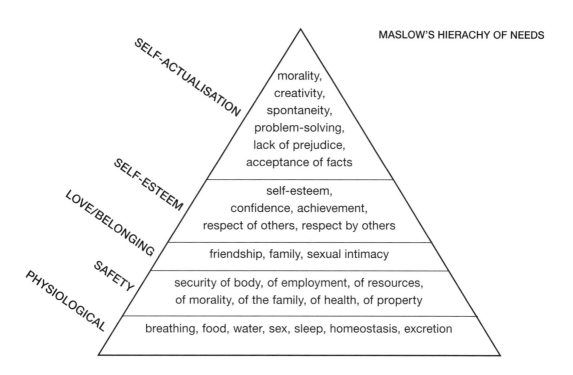

MASLOW'S HIERACHY OF NEEDS

SELF-ACTUALISATION
SELF-ESTEEM
LOVE/BELONGING
SAFETY
PHYSIOLOGICAL

morality,
creativity,
spontaneity,
problem-solving,
lack of prejudice,
acceptance of facts

self-esteem,
confidence, achievement,
respect of others, respect by others

friendship, family, sexual intimacy

security of body, of employment, of resources,
of morality, of the family, of health, of property

breathing, food, water, sex, sleep, homeostasis, excretion

Essentially, as we all know from experience, if we are hungry or cold, feel worried or stressed, concentrating on tasks and actually 'learning' in a formal sense is very difficult. We are probably all aware of the logic and common sense of this, and yet on any given day in our classrooms there may be children who are hungry (child poverty is increasing - in 2014 - 15 there were an estimated 3.9 million children living in poverty - Child Poverty Action Group (CPAG) 2016 - that is 9 in a class of 30, or 28% of children). They may be tired, worried about parents, or siblings, wondering who will be in their home at the end of the day, wondering where their home may be, anxious about when they may next see a parent or sibling, or even traumatised from witnessing or experiencing violence, neglect or abuse. Those children will find it hard to concentrate on individual tasks or the business of learning. Often they are expected to continue going to school when adults in their position would, without any doubt, be signed off sick and possibly medicated.

I am sure everyone reading this will have had an experience when they have found it very hard to learn or indeed concentrate on anything. The reasons vary: simple things, as I've mentioned, like being cold or hungry, too tired or in pain will mean it is hard to focus on anything other than the temperature, hunger, tiredness or pain. Sometimes this is easy to fix: a simple painkiller may deal with a headache, for example, although problems like appendicitis will not be remedied until there is surgery. In addition to medical or physical problems, there are a whole host of other reasons why learning can be tough. If we are worried, we find our concentration drifting in and out of the task in hand. We will all have spent time reading something only to realise, as we turn the page, that our mind has been elsewhere and we haven't attended to a word of the text.

As adults, significant problems such as the illness of a loved one, bereavement, break-up of a relationship or worry about redundancy will all have an impact on our ability, not only to concentrate, but perhaps to even function effectively. So too may an impending lesson observation, a looming inspection, a row with someone, a new manager, or even an exam. Yet we expect children to come to school and behave appropriately without the years of experience that we as adults have had in learning to cope with and manage the torrent of emotions we experience at such times. Some of the children and young people in our classes may be coping with situations that are far more distressing than the things which cause us to 'go to pieces'.

Recently I worked with a 15 year old young woman whose foster placement had broken down. Quite literally when Zorshca came to school one day, which happened to be in a specialist setting, she did not know where her home would be that evening.

Moving home is ranked as one of the most stressful life experiences that exist for adults, though as adults, we can usually exert some control in the form of choice. Yet Zorscha came to school and then within minutes problems arose; she refused to hand in her phone because she wanted to access her messages. Wouldn't we all need our phones at such times? Even within a specialist setting there didn't seem to be the structures in place to support her through a troubling time when her basic needs in terms of security simply hadn't been met.

Of course if the phone hadn't been the problem, probably there would have been something else. Part of Zorscha was understandably struggling to get her basic needs for security met and have a way of expressing her anxiety. Her chance of learning in any formal sense was hampered by her need to ensure she would be alright.

It may be helpful for a moment just to consider how you and your own setting would manage this sort of situation, perhaps making an exception to the usual practice to meet a particular need. Of course normality and routine can sometimes provide a bit of a relief, providing an escape from certain problems. We've probably all had that experience as well - work as a distraction from other problematic areas of our lives. School can be a calming and even therapeutic environment for children experiencing distress. But we also need to acknowledge that sometimes simply being in school and just about holding it together will take every ounce of strength and resilience a child or young person has, and there may simply not be enough energy left to focus on learning. We also need to be aware that when they are in this position, children and young people are vulnerable to all sorts of triggers, making them react unpredictably to peers, staff and the environment.

***Ashley** (15) had been sent out of class for falling asleep. Staff knew he was from a background with substantial social care support. In the support centre he said that he felt exhausted but questioning revealed little: he just said he had 'stuff going on'. He wasn't in school the next day, and we later found that he had been sent to another area for a time to stay with his aunt, as his mother, who was known to have mental health problems, had been hospitalised again.*

His simple statement that he 'had stuff going on' was a massive underestimate of the trauma he was experiencing. Maybe he couldn't articulate it, maybe he didn't want to. But it was not at all surprising, with hindsight, that he had spent most of his day in the behaviour support unit within the school, often in a state of semi-sleep. Sleep is one way that the body can shut down and is an acknowledged response in some individuals to stress.

Looking back I wonder what he learned that day, not just at school but in terms of his whole situation. I imagine he learned that life is unpredictable; that it can change dramatically; that you can be separated very quickly from people you love: that people you love can change, and maybe that the emotions that go with such experiences are not nice, or maybe that they need to be squashed down in some way. I suppose we will never know, but giving a place for people like Ashley to have a voice and express his worries seems something which is absolutely essential for schools to provide. I spent some time afterwards wondering what would have helped me most if I had been in his position; but of course even imagining the distress and disempowerment he must have felt was almost impossible.

Learning outside school

School staff are also aware that our pupils are not just learning when they are with us at school - of course they are also learning at home. While we may hazard guesses, we can never really know what is being learned there either. And it's complex. Children and young people's behaviour and readiness to learn may give an indication of what is happening at home. But of course some behaviour may stem from particular individual difficulties the pupil has (for example a specific learning difficulty such as dyspraxia), rather than what is being experienced at home. But clearly, there will be a relationship between these areas.

Learning from others

All the experiences children and young people have will be teaching them things about the world, other people, and themselves. They may not of course be learning things that will help them in a school environment, but they may well be learning. Learning often takes place when it may not be intended. Watching how someone else copes with a problem can give us strategies to try when we face a similar situation: conversely, seeing other people exhibiting a fear of something may implant a sense of wariness in us that hadn't been there before. Some children may have seen siblings struggle with school, truant, or be excluded - undoubtedly they will learn something from this, and from parental and school responses to such events.

Lewis was 11 and his education was provided by a medical needs team, as he had a diagnosis of school phobia and high anxiety. He had two older siblings who were over 16. Both of these siblings had also spent a considerable time out of school though their diagnosis varied. Not one of them had gone to a school prom, neither had sat GCSE's and neither were working or studying at the time of my involvement.

His older brother and sister and indeed Lewis may have had definite medical, psychological or socio-emotional conditions, but Lewis had probably also absorbed a message that in his family, it wasn't essential to go to school.

Children may also be learning things that an adult would not want a child to learn, like sensing when someone is going to get angry or violent and learning to make themselves scarce, or eating as much as they can, possibly even taking and hiding food when it's there, because they have learned it may be a long time till they are offered food again.

Justin was seven when I worked with him. He was a live wire, with a very sharp sense of humour and was open to every new experience that was put in front of him: theatre trips, sport, and art. But sadly, his behaviour meant he couldn't always take part in certain activities.

He did manage to get on a theatre trip, through which he chatted non-stop and bounced on his seat with joy like a two year old. During the interval, Justin said to me, "Miss, I don't mean to be bad, I just am - even when I am trying not to be!"

Justin was always late, frequently smelled, was always hungry and would steal from lunch boxes if he had the chance. His family was well known to social services. He was often disruptive in lessons, found it hard to concentrate and had learned a whole range of tactics to avoid doing any work at all.

Justin was an active engaging child with a thirst for knowledge, but whose attention span was shorter than that of a two year old. Justin learned 'facts' easily and enjoyed 'sharing' these with anyone and everyone. Sadly, Justin had also learned that he was 'bad'. The hope is that no-one in a school setting had said that: it may have been said at home, or maybe he had just 'figured out' that was how he was viewed by some. Seeing himself in that way continued to have an impact on Justin, who went on to face immense difficulties, as he was taken into care and rocketed through a number of different placements.

For the type of learning we want to happen in school, bearing Maslow's Hierarchy in mind will help us to understand why some children can't always be ready to learn. Even when they do turn up in our schools, it may be a case of them being there in body but not having the emotional, social or psychological resources to truly access learning, through no fault of their own. If all children and young people arrived at school well rested, well-fed, clothed appropriately and with a string of loving, supportive adults around them who nurtured their self-esteem and gave them the confidence to try new things, even if that means they risked failure, then working in a school would genuinely be a pleasure and a privilege. And it is: because that is the case for some of our pupils, some of the time. In some schools, it is possibly the case for most of the pupils, most of the time. But sadly it is not the experience of all. Working with those children is a privilege and can be a pleasure too, but of a very different nature.

A safe place to learn

Issues to do with how we see ourselves can also have an impact on our readiness to learn. Most of us would feel distracted and uncomfortable if we thought we might be the butt of jokes or ridicule; some pupils experience teasing and worse because of appearance, clothes, weight or possessions. No-one likes to look silly, though some children and young people may use that as a strategy to deflect from other emotions; for example, the young person who is misbehaving, perhaps playing the class clown to get out of doing work that may be too hard because understandably, no-one likes to look unintelligent. Deciding to act in a silly way can be an active choice. Both instances may lead to ridicule from peers, and as I noted earlier, bullying was reported as a problem for almost half of those surveyed by *Ditch the Label* (*see* p.16). But being the student in the class who makes everyone laugh may also give a certain status among peers.

Nowadays children and young people may be painfully aware that what happens in class is not necessarily left there when they go home, but may be broadcast or commented on via social media. In a poll of 11 - 17 year olds (Guardian 2014) 35% said they had experienced cyberbullying, compared with 16% in the previous year; and four in ten said they had witnessed others being bullied online.

Human beings function well when we feel confident in our environment, accepted by the people around us and have a sense that we belong: we saw this above in Maslow's Hierarchy. So in addition to the children who may be experiencing problems outside school, significant numbers of children find school itself the problem. Many pupils worry about the work they have to do. They worry about others making fun of them, or the feeling of frustration and failure that comes with being unable to do the work that is presented, and significant numbers experience bullying. They may have previous experience of finding things difficult, of getting things wrong, which, let's be honest, is not fun.

REFLECTIVE ACTIVITY

⇨   Think about something you hate doing, and that you know you are not brilliant at. Maybe navigating, speaking a foreign language, dealing with new technology? Just try to think about the emotions you feel when you are put in a situation where you have to perform this task.
Then think about doing it in front of others who can all do it better than you.

⇨   Note down some of the emotions this stirs up for you.

⇨   Then think about what would improve the experience - what support you could be given so it that it might become a positive experience.

Children and young people are no different to adults in this respect: they too feel anxious, worried and may try almost anything to get out of the situation.

Emily was dyslexic but achieved a 'C' in GCSE English. She told me after she had left school that her overriding memory of English lessons (which she had always appeared to enjoy and she had certainly never been a difficult student) was of panic, 'blind panic', whenever there was a lesson where the class would read aloud. She would frantically try to work out what section she would have to read and practise, so could never listen to what the others were reading. And of course the order might change unexpectedly, causing her even more panic.

Emily was an intelligent student, but at 16, when you can't read simple words, you feel ashamed (her words). Even though teachers may understand, even other pupils may understand, it's exposing to have your difficulty publicly paraded. She said she felt ashamed, stupid and ridiculous. "What I wanted every time was for the fire bell to go off or someone to faint … anything just to avoid the inevitable feeling of humiliation."

Emily was actually on the gifted and talented register of the school: she was in school plays, she was well liked and had a supportive group of friends. But it wasn't just reading aloud. In primary school, spelling tests were a huge issue for her, and even at 16 she told me how it angered her to have homework returned with spellings corrected in red by all the teachers who actually knew that she was dyslexic. Emily hated being allowed extra time for exams, which again made public that she was one of those who couldn't read well, one of the slow ones. In her eyes all extra time did was prolong the agony of being placed in a situation where humiliation was likely.

She also told me how much she hated being taken out of lessons for support: she argued that she didn't want this, but of course the school had wanted to be supportive. Again Emily spoke of dread as the time approached, and she had to remind the teacher that she had to leave for 'special lessons'. As she left she said she would just hope she didn't miss anything that was fun, or where she may have had the chance to do something that she would have liked but people might have forgotten to include her. Then later she would try with the skill of a detective to track down the work missed and make sure it was covered.

I admire young people like Emily, and there are many like her who each day feel trepidation when they approach learning: yet they put themselves through this each day, cope with the frustrations and somehow actually manage to learn.

__Tom__ was very different. He had a number of learning needs and hated being put in a position where he had to write in class. So he would start some argument as the task was being given out and escalate this to the point of being sent out. This would result in detentions, but, as he told me later, that while this may have made him look difficult, it didn't make him look 'thick'.

Tom had supportive parents who had lost count of the times they had been called into school. Tom had also been identified as dyslexic, and he developed a whole raft of strategies to avoid the situations where he might look 'thick'. Again, he was a popular boy with a good group of supportive peers, many of whom were high achievers. He never truanted: in fact he told me he enjoyed the social side of school. It was the writing (and reading) that he hated, which of course were requirements for almost every lesson. He

achieved eight GCSE's at 'C' or above, but if he had been able to complete his exams orally
he might well have achieved more 'A's.

One of the advantages many people have cited about online learning courses is that you never have to look silly in front of others. None of us like being the one who doesn't know. If children are worrying about the next worksheet, or the comment a member of staff or another pupil may make, they will find it harder to learn. Through these experiences, our children and young people will be developing internal 'scripts' - *"You are no good"*, *"You are stupid"*, *"You will fail again"*, or similar. These will be replayed and in themselves may prove to be a block to further learning. But perhaps most destructive of all are the emotions our pupils feel, which may be a physical sensation or a feeling of shame or sadness, and unsurprisingly, may lead a child or young person to avoid such situations of distress - and thus learning - in future.

The effects of bullying

The nearly 26,000 children who had a counselling session about bullying (NSPCC 2016) were the ones who picked up the phone, so it seems safe to assume that many more may have felt bullied or felt anxiety about bullying but couldn't or didn't reach out. That's a lot of pupils in a lot of classrooms who simply weren't feeling safe. As we've seen, worrying about something may rob us of the focus we need to learn. Sustained worry or stress can cause all sorts of problems, and we know that the experience of being bullied may have a severe impact on the health and wellbeing of individuals even into later life. It can impact our pupils' self-esteem and their confidence. Regrettably evidence suggests it also makes them more like to become victims in the future, while the bullies were more likely to grow up as adult criminals (Farrington et al, 2009). It can certainly mean that these pupils won't be ready to learn. It's vitally important that regardless of what is happening outside school, that inside, our pupils and students feel safe and secure enough to learn.

IN SUMMARY

In this chapter, we have looked at learning, at the way children are programmed for learning, at learning styles and areas of informal learning in addition to the curriculum. We've also considered Maslow's Hierarchy of Needs and the way that a child or young person's needs and experiences will have an impact on their readiness to learn.

▶ In schools, we can rarely fix lives: school staff are not miracle workers or even social workers. We may be able to offer support, alert other agencies and ameliorate some of our pupils' problems to an extent, when they come to our attention. But the pupil who has a parent with a mental health problem or an addiction, or the child who is being abused, or being bullied, or struggling with work, may spend a lot of time in the classroom with their problems and emotions filling their minds so they are simply not ready to learn. They may feel anxious, worried, ill, distressed or in pain. They may have times when their body is flooded with stress chemicals that cause them to behave in particularly challenging ways. They may seem stuck in a fearful, sad, isolated and lonely place.

▶ Schools may not be able to put many of these things right, but we can create an environment where the pupil feels safe and cared for: we can make schools into places that are compassionate and nurturing. Hopefully, at the very least, we can respond to our pupils in a way which doesn't make the problems worse. Learning to respond to such pupils in a supportive way is not only good for the pupil. It will actually help the whole school by minimising the disruption that may be caused by someone who is not in a state to learn, as well as providing indirect learning for everyone on how to relate to someone who is stressed. We can create school environments and cultures that are supportive for every child and every adult within that school.

▶ In the next chapter I'll start to consider the context in which learning takes place, and how, with the right culture, attitudes and language, we can create environments that will help children and young people be ready to learn.

MAIN POINTS

✓ There are different areas of learning and different styles of learning.

✓ There are certain needs that must be met before individuals are ready to learn.

✓ Creating an environment that is compassionate and nurturing will ensure that disruption to learning is minimised and that every individual feels valued.

✓ Classrooms that feel safe for all pupils will create the best and most secure environment for learning for everyone.

CHAPTER 2

Creating a context for learning

A culture of care

Schools are places of learning, but they are also places of care. As school staff, we accept the statutory duty of care we have for the children and young people within our school environment. We saw in Chapter 1 that learning is likely to be more effective when pupils feel cared for and secure.

REFLECTIVE ACTIVITY

⇨ Imagine yourself as a visitor in your school.
   What things would tell you about the culture of the school?

⇨ How was that culture created?

⇨ Would everyone in the school, staff, students, parents and visitors, describe the same culture?

⇨ Would the caretaker or mealtime supervisors experience the same culture as others?

⇨ Would all parents describe a similar culture?

We would probably all say that we'd want our schools to radiate a culture of care, be places of welcome, nurture and acceptance. But is that culture actually communicated to everyone who attends, works or visits the school? And if not, what do we need to change?

Culture is hard to define but we're all aware of it. All sorts of different things contribute to the culture, from the displays in the foyer to the mission statement. Every single interaction and action that occurs can reveal something about the institution and the values that are represented.

Culture can be defined in a few different ways but when we are thinking of the culture of an organisation we usually take it to mean the *values and beliefs* of the organisation, which are reflected in the *policies, behaviours and actions of the people* within that organisation. The *physical environment* can also give a message about the culture, but that in itself is determined by people, and reflected in the policies, procedures, displays and any communication which take place within or from the organisation.

> ***I had*** *an unhappy experience recently visiting my sister. She is blind and has a learning disability, and was in hospital following a fall in which she broke her arm. As I walked to the ward I saw several patient charters and value or mission statements, which gave the message that people would be treated as individuals with care and courtesy.*
>
> *What I found was entirely different. My sister was slumped in a bed with a drink she would not be able to pick up - hours after her operation, still in a gown, food stains around her mouth. I summoned a nurse who spoke to me, not to my sister, telling me she hadn't eaten much. I explained that she would need assistance to feed herself. She would routinely need food cutting up, placing within easy reach and would usually eat from a plate with a guard. I imagine, despite the lengthy forms the staff from her care home had completed on her admission, that no-one had read about her specific care needs. A cup of tea was offered -which would have been a struggle for her to drink on her own: she usually uses an ordinary cup but having to use her left arm would be a new challenge. The tea never arrived, so after 30 minutes and two reminders, I went to get one for her myself from the canteen.*

The culture I witnessed was inconsiderate and unprofessional at best, and callous and uncaring at worst. It lacked empathy or even a willingness to try and understand the needs of a patient on a general ward with 'special' needs. The culture of every organisation is tangible, true in schools as it is in hospital. The real culture is experienced by everyone who works or visits or 'uses' the organisation. And in many cases it is characterised by the stated values of the organisation.

REFLECTIVE ACTIVITY

⇨   Think about some recent interactions within your school. This could
       be with students or pupils, colleagues, managers, visitors or parents.

⇨   How were the values of the school expressed in those interactions?

⇨   Were they positive - did they accurately reflect what the school
       has identified as essential in value terms?

⇨   If not - why not?

⇨   What would have made a real difference?

It's easier in most cases to have a mission statement that says within the school 'everyone will feel valued' than it is to ensure this is the case on a day when there are staff off sick, stress levels are high because of impending inspections, or there are a few particularly difficult parents in the playground. It can help to identify situations that go wrong, and then analyse why. We know when we don't feel valued, and usually, most of us know when an interaction has left others feeling undervalued, or criticised. These are the times to really examine what happened, why it happened and importantly, what could have been done differently (*and see* p.40).

In my experience in schools where staff are working with vulnerable or troubled children, cultures cascade. If a member of staff feels valued and supported, if they feel that they matter, that someone is looking out for them, they are better able to withstand the demands of working with children who are troubled. All but the newest members of a staff team will have experienced different styles of management. It's interesting to think for a moment about our own experiences.

> **REFLECTIVE ACTIVITY**
>
> ⇨ Think of a time when you felt well managed.
>
> ⇨ What specific aspects of management helped you feel this?

Sometimes it's the level of support we receive that makes all the difference to how we feel. If the level of support is good, then even if we feel too busy, and challenged by some of the roles we're trying to fulfil, we can keep going because we know the support is there, and if we need more help we can ask without fear of reproach or criticism. Sometimes the sense of respect a person has for the experience of the manager also creates a sense of understanding (they have been here, they understand).

But equally, we need to be aware that what one person may see as support, another may see as interference. Many staff complain about a lack of autonomy to simply get on with the job. Increasingly these days, autonomy is seen as a rarity within schools, where it seems the government, Ofsted and a whole host of others have ideas and standards that are put upon teachers and other education professionals. The current government approach is to allow more autonomy with regard to school management. But staff in many schools don't appear to feel they work as autonomous professionals, feeling instead they work to ever tighter guidelines with an increasing number of boxes to tick.

Most people who work in schools want to do a good job. They want to have the resources to do this and they want to be valued as individuals and respected by those they work with. If staff teams feel they are cared for, and work within a culture of care, they are more likely to be able to cope with the rigors of teaching and working with the children and young people who themselves need high levels of care and whose behaviour may cause difficulties within their classroom.

Staff who are well managed within teams and feel valued will be less likely to suffer stress. The case study below shows this working in one setting.

Tabitha was a newly qualified teacher working in a primary school, and Surinder was the teaching assistant who worked with Malik, a seven year old with numerous difficulties who was in the class. Malik was on the autistic spectrum, and was one of three children on the cusp of going into care as his single parent mother, who struggled to manage his behaviour, was truly at the end of her tether. He was undergoing an assessment to identify his needs more accurately, as it was apparent from the level of challenging behaviour he exhibited that the current setting was not able to meet them all.

But of course assessments take time, and while some of his behaviour, which could be quite violent, could easily have 'justified' exclusions, the school was aware that an exclusion to home would almost certainly precipitate Malik going into care.

On one particular visit to the school I spoke with Tabitha and Surinder about how they were coping. They both immediately said they couldn't keep going without each other, and then mentioned several things they did like debriefing after any incidents and using this to adjust plans for the next day. We talked some more and it became obvious that the timetable had been amended to enable Tabitha and Surinder a half lesson slot for debrief at the end of the school day whilst Malik was supported working on the computer - an activity he loved, and whilst the rest of the class joined with another for their literacy/story session covered by the Head or deputy.

In this case the whole school had worked together to help the frontline staff cope with what was an extreme and fairly unusual situation. The result was that they felt valued and supported and able to carry on teaching and supporting Malik. Surely it would be to everyone's advantage for all schools to have this kind of culture of care? Yet it seems apparent when I talk to some staff, students and parents this it is simply not the case. So it seems crucial for us to think through how an effective atmosphere of care can be created and maintained.

Effective cultures of care

There are many elements that contribute to the creation of a caring culture. I suggest the ones I've identified below are essential, but the list is certainly not exhaustive. In many ways if the first is embedded and every individual truly is valued, the rest may well fall into place.

> **A CULTURE THAT VALUES EVERY INDIVIDUAL**
> **A CULTURE OF RESPECT, COURTESY AND KINDNESS**
> **A CULTURE OF TOLERANCE (NO BLAME) AND CHALLENGE**
> **A CULTURE THAT IS OPEN, HONEST AND TRANSPARENT**

1   A CULTURE THAT VALUES EVERY INDIVIDUAL

Feeling valued is something that's hard to measure. Often it's about someone noticing what you do or, more importantly perhaps, noticing you. That you stayed late again, brought in the coffee again, or that you've changed hairstyle; small personal things in addition to the measurable outcomes about progress or lesson observations. It's true that often a simple thank you, when sincere, can count for a lot.

> ## REFLECTIVE ACTIVITY
> ⇨   Think about a recent situation where you felt valued, appreciated, or even noticed in a positive way.
> ⇨   What was it that made you feel that: a comment, an action or something else?
> ⇨   Now think about a time when you did not feel noticed, valued or appreciated.
> ⇨   Why did you not feel valued in that situation?

We have all seen or heard the slogan 'if you can't say something positive then don't say anything at all'. Obviously there is a place for constructive criticism, for holding people to account and for challenge. But in schools sometimes we think carefully about what we may say to children or young people, but don't afford the same courtesy to colleagues. Try making a conscious decision to say something positive to at least five people every day, and see the difference that it can make.

The important thing about a culture that values individuals is that *the value is inherent in the individual.* Each person is valued simply because he or she is an individual human being. We often feel valued when people notice our efforts, or work, but a genuine culture of value is about valuing each person simply for the fact of being human. In my experience, cultures where such value is authentic support strong working relationships, where the adults trust one another. An effective, caring culture does not mean staff have to be close friends outside the school environment, though caring about individuals often means that something about their life outside school is known. If we value a person we value 'them', that individual with their own joys and problems, not just what they do between 8am and 4pm. It's often hard to think about how that value can be communicated - but it can be, and many of us have been privileged to work in cultures where that's the case in reality, not just something that appears in a mission statement or charter.

At the same time, sadly, we have probably all seen examples when a destructive, uncaring or bullying culture has had tragic consequences, because even as new people join they either 'succumb' to the culture or, as is often the case, leave. Unhelpful cultures can and should be challenged, which may be difficult and may involve putting your head above the parapet. Uncaring cultures hurt people. Working or learning in a culture that is not caring damages people. The extent and nature of the damage may vary but it hurts when we are not valued, not seen as worthy of respect, when we don't have our feelings, opinions or ideas listened to, when we are expected to stay late to perform tasks that aren't part of our role, or when we are simply not noticed. I have sadly come across a number of teachers and teaching assistants who no longer work in schools. Their reason for leaving was not the children or young people, but the cultures which they felt were demeaning, uncaring and unsupportive: in short, cultures that didn't value the individual. If they continue unchallenged, such cultures don't simply damage staff, they damage children and may cause additional trauma for vulnerable children and young people.

However, the good news is that where there is a good culture, new people joining witness the acceptance and care and begin to mirror this. If someone joins the team who doesn't exhibit the core values, it will become apparent, and usually they will change or leave.

2   A CULTURE OF RESPECT, COURTESY AND KINDNESS

We seem to live in a society that demands respect as a right, but we also hear that respect must be earned. Surely every human being deserves to be treated with respect, regardless of any other consideration? That seems to be a natural follow-on from valuing individuals. Identifying exactly how we can show respect can initially seem hard, and again it might help to think about the things others can do or say to us that can help us feel respected, starting from what works. Respect is defined in some dictionaries as 'esteem' for people, simply holding a belief that they matter, that they have value, and ensuring that our behaviour reflects that belief. As someone who visits many schools I notice a lot of differences in how respect is or isn't expressed. In some schools I visit, even if I have never been there before, there is a friendly smile, perhaps a little conversation. If I need to wait I will be shown where I can wait comfortably, perhaps offered a drink, as well as guided on completing all the essentials, like signing in and being given an ID badge. We have no problem knowing when we have been treated respectfully. But we also know about being treated disrespectfully. Because the converse can also happen: it's sometimes a curt *"Come in"*, being left standing in the corridor, not being told when I am likely to see the person I have come to visit, perhaps even being forgotten about for some time. And of course it can be much worse: people may be ignored, talked over and even discriminated against, none of which would happen if there was respect.

We hear about respect a lot now; even the word 'respect' is used as a greeting between some young people, and I'm sure, every rapper has at some point rapped about it. Respect in many ways is an attitude of mind - the actions or attributes which *show* respect are often courtesy or kindness. But these are both words which aren't talked about so much: we do hear a lot about assertiveness and rights. Where the word 'care' can imply a level of responsibility, 'kindness' seems more about benevolence, indulgence, consideration, doing something not because we have a duty to but because we want to. Shakespeare (in Macbeth) speaks of the 'milk of human kindness': kindness is nourishing, it makes things flow a little more smoothly. Importantly, as an attitude, it can be present even in situations where there is conflict.

> *I witnessed* both the following scenes in a supermarket. The first toddler grabbed *something from a shelf (a multibag of crisps) and was immediately shouted at. The crisps were roughly tugged from the child's hand, and he was then half dragged away by his mother who continued her tirade about his behaviour while the little boy cried loudly.*
>
> *The second toddler was at the checkout with mum and repeatedly whining for sweets which were on the belt. In a calm voice, the mother said at least twice, and on one occasion bending very close to the child, that the child could have the sweets in the car provided that she stopped whining. The child continued her high pitched whine. As the mother pushed the trolley loaded with shopping, she stroked the child's head and said that she wouldn't be getting the sweets because she was still whining.*

This is not meant to be a commentary on parenting style, simply an example to demonstrate that even when enforcing boundaries or disciplining a child, there can be kindness. Other than to attract attention (often over a hubbub of noise) or give a sudden warning (a child about to touch something hot for example) there can never really be an excuse for shouting at either an adult or a child - it is not kind, courteous or effective. For children who are troubled it may be the norm outside school (or it may not), but it will usually cause an unfavourable reaction. Neither is it kind to humiliate anyone - though in some schools it seems that while some of the behaviour strategies may not be *designed* to humiliate, that is one of the side effects.

As an adult and as a member of staff, it's worth periodically walking through the behaviour policy 'as a child' to consider the impact of the strategies or sanctions. How would it feel to be stood outside the head's office, made to stand, sit in a specific place, to be separated from friends? I am not at all saying these things should never be done. Schools need ways to correct or discipline, but it is always worth considering how the strategies we set up fit within the culture of the school, how they can be delivered with respect and kindness, and how they may be experienced by the individual child or young person.

Of course sometimes staff feel they are not treated with kindness or respect by colleagues, managers, children, young people or by other members of the pupils' families! Hopefully not from colleagues, but we may have to endure being shouted at, sworn at, ignored, insulted, criticised or belittled in front of others, even physically assaulted by pupils or indeed by parents.

In situations where people *external* to the school are involved in being disrespectful to employees or others in the school - relatives of pupils, for example, then the reaction (while respectful) must be emphatic about the need to show respect. Then there will need to be a proactive approach to stop future incidents happening.

In families where shouting is commonplace, the tendency can be for the volume and intensity to increase when situations are tense. Not only is this ineffective but it doesn't take long before everyone is shouting all the time. The same is true, as we know, with respect. Even if we are presented with anger, rudeness or abuse, if we persist in meeting it with respect rather than anger, which can increase the conflict, situations are likely to be less damaging and resolved more quickly.

I have worked with schools where some staff feel supported, valued and treated with kindness, and others in the same staff team feel almost the opposite. In one particular school the divide wasn't between support staff and teachers, but between staff who lived in or near the village where the school was situated, and those who did not. There was a high level of informal communication outside school which left some staff feeling outside the loop, that their opinions were not of value and that they were not privy to important information; just one example of what happens when an 'in-group' forms. Clearly, respect is vital; disrespect must be challenged at every opportunity, and the culture discussed within the staff room in both a formal and informal way.

In every organisation there needs to be some way of checking the internal 'temperature' with regard to how people are feeling. An annual staff survey won't really be enough. There needs to be some regular time when people can at least be given the opportunity to say what they feel and be listened to. In a culture of respect, everybody's opinion matters: people have the chance to think together about how the situation can be changed or improved. This takes courage, and may take time, but in the end, creating a culture where every individual is respected will pay dividends. In theory, if a culture exists where individuals are valued and treated with respect, there simply should be no need for anti-discriminatory policies (though I think they need to exist as an additional safeguard) because to discriminate in any way is not to value or treat with respect.

When I look back at the different environments I've worked in, often what made it a good job, one I have stayed in and enjoyed, was the culture of the organisation. This probably counted even more than the children or young people I was working with, enjoyable and rewarding though that was. When the staff team feels valued, trust each other and can treat others and be treated with respect and kindness, then even if the job is tough and challenging, the hours long and the workload heavy, somehow we can find satisfaction.

> ## REFLECTIVE ACTIVITY
>
> ⇨   Identify an environment you have worked in where you did NOT feel respected, noticed, valued or appreciated - then a couple of examples of situations or actions that made you feel that way.
>
> ⇨   Now think of an environment you have worked in where you DID feel respected - then give some examples of the situations or actions that made you feel that way. What was it that made you feel that: a comment, an action or something else? I imagine that they weren't big or difficult things to achieve yet the impact can be immense.

3   A CULTURE OF TOLERANCE (NO BLAME) AND CHALLENGE

A culture of no blame is essential to make sure people feel able to try new things, admit when things go wrong and ask for support. Sadly the need for this has been highlighted a great deal in the news recently following tragic events within hospitals. Accountability is of course important, and it can co-exist with tolerance. Taking responsibility for something and being accountable is something staff in schools are all too familiar with, and indeed they are often blamed for things which are well beyond their control. Clearly schools need systems in place to make sure staff feel supported, able to ask for help, and can admit if they don't know what to do in a given situation or feel they have made some kind of error.

School managers need a system of regular appraisals to tackle any particular difficulties, but it is my general belief that folk who want an easy life generally do not choose to work in schools. There will always be exceptions, but most people who work in schools usually do so because they like people in general, children in particular and get some sense of satisfaction, if not excitement, about the process of learning and development. Sometimes a bad job is done, but often it is because a person feels ill-equipped and ill-supported, or is possibly just in the wrong niche. All of these can be remedied *if* the culture is one that can offer care and support to staff as well as to the pupils and students. It's worth repeating that staff need to be nurtured and cared for in order to continue nurturing and caring for their pupils.

Sometimes the shortcomings are within management which compounds the frustration and stress that staff dealing with troubled children and young people feel. If this is the case then it is imperative that colleagues are supportive to each other and that deficiencies are highlighted in an appropriate and professional manner. Ignoring problems of management rarely means they go away: usually staff leave, which increases the pressure on staff who stay, and the culture remains the same. However, having a 'no blame' culture doesn't mean that there can't be challenge. Blame is what makes people say *"You did wrong - it's your fault"*. Challenge says, *"What happened, and how could things have been done differently?"* or even *"That* (whether an action or a word or even an attitude) *doesn't fit well with the culture we have here."* We often hear negative comments about political correctness and how sometimes it's thought to be too extreme. But we need it because thoughts, attitudes and words are what can ultimately drive actions. A discriminatory comment or joke must be challenged or the discriminatory attitudes behind it may be accepted, and in turn this may lead to actions that are discriminatory. Humour is an important part of human relationships but if hearing jokes or comments in the staff room or anywhere else makes you hope that someone else doesn't hear what's being said, then maybe a challenge is needed to someone, or even to yourself.

Challenge is not the same as criticism. Challenge can be supportive, and importantly, it can bring improvement and change when it's made within a culture of care. Challenge is an important part of improving performance and if we work in schools it is really important that we improve to be the best we can be, which will happen when there is challenge. But for challenge to spur us on rather than make us feel got at, it must happen in a culture that is tolerant and not one which blames the individual.

Try this activity: it won't need to be shared with anyone, so you can be as honest with yourself as possible.

> ## REFLECTIVE ACTIVITY
>
> ⇨   Think about a situation where things didn't go well for you, a lesson,
>   dealing with a challenging situation or conflict with a colleague.
>   Reflect on this as honestly as you can and particularly the contribution you
>   made to it not being an effective or helpful episode.
>
> ⇨   Why did you act in the way you did? Was it because you felt out of
>   your depth, lacking knowledge, or feeling stressed about something else?
>
> ⇨   What would have helped you do things differently - and why did these
>   things NOT happen?
>
> ⇨   What could you put in place NOW to help you deal better with a similar
>   situation in future?
>
> ⇨   Lastly, just spend a minute thinking about ways tolerance AND challenge
>   could be used to improve your own practice.

4   A CULTURE THAT IS OPEN, HONEST AND TRANSPARENT

This seems in many ways a follow-on from valuing the individual, showing respect and
challenging rather than blaming. There are obviously occasions when confidentiality is
important. At times, there are real reasons why information should only be shared on a
need-to-know basis, and it is part of valuing individuals and treating them with respect
that we maintain these boundaries. But sometimes knowledge can be a burden, and
unlike other organisations where there are effective supervision systems, staff in schools
sometimes feel they must shoulder the burdens alone. It is important that staff are honest
with others and with children and young people, but that too can sometimes feel onerous:
knowing, for example, that a child may soon be moving from one foster placement to
another but being asked not to tell the child, may well cause stress for the adults in the
situation, who can find themselves in circumstances where even if not directly lying, they
are forced to be economical with the truth. At such times it is important that staff can
acknowledge how challenging this can be. Good staff care would also mean that they
could have space to discuss how they are feeling with someone else, if they wish.

There are definitely occasions when information is sensitive and, in order to respect the child or other members of their family, certain details should not be discussed. But there are times when some information needs to be shared (perhaps without many details) so that there can be support for those involved in the situation. As with other aspects of culture, sometimes our actions don't live up to our words. We are human and will experience a whole range of emotions on any given day. Often our experience may have been that we must hide these emotions, and carry on regardless. But a culture of openness and honesty can be a safeguard for everyone. All too often when there are tragedies, the investigations reveal a lack of transparency; people had concerns that either weren't expressed or listened to.

A culture of honesty and transparency is not incompatible with the safeguarding of sensitive information when this is done within a culture that values every individual. In such a culture people can be honest about their needs, and if they need support, and this means that certain information must be shared, then that is a legitimate reason. In general I think the recourse to 'confidentiality' is over-used. Information may be sensitive, but professional staff within schools must be trusted to manage sensitive information with respect for the individuals concerned.

If you are fortunate enough to work in a culture that values individuals and respects them, one that doesn't blame but challenges and is open and transparent, then guard it jealously. Such a culture will benefit everyone within the organisation, and can demonstrate new ways of relating and reacting to others for children who may have experienced situations and environments that are very different. Be explicit about the culture of your school, explain why things are done the way they are. This will help children and young people see that there are different ways of managing themselves and relationships. And at the same time, be aware that this difference in perspective may be very difficult for them to come to terms with and may even create conflicts along the way. After all, if adults who are not related to a child value and treat him with respect, when for a whole variety of reasons his own parents or others may not have been able to do so, then many different wounds may be opened up before the emotional healing, which comes about from being valued, can begin.

Getting the environment right

We all know that our environment has an impact on us. It's why when we decorate our homes, we choose colours that we like and fill rooms with items that aren't just functional but make us feel good as well. Putting effort into the environment will not solve all the problems in a school, but may help staff and vulnerable pupils feel more secure.

This section considers mostly the classroom or learning environment, but each part of the school environment is important. Staff who have a place to relax (even briefly) or have meetings with teachers or other professionals, who have areas where they can work and talk to pupils on an individual basis, will find their job easier than those who don't have access to such facilities. Space is at a premium in many primary schools in particular, and it isn't unusual to come across children working in corridors. Clearly there are restraints, but it's important to recognise that the physical environment has an impact on everyone in the school, and there's probably always something we can do to improve it.

A visitor, or angry parent, who walks in and is given a place to wait that is comfortable and pleasant will have a different perception of the school to someone who has to stand in a corridor. In so many ways the environment truly is an expression of the school culture. If it's one of care, where individuals are valued, then effort and resources will be allocated to ensure their comfort, an essential part of valuing people.

REFLECTIVE ACTIVITY

⇨   Next time you enter your school building in the middle of the day, try to
      see it as if you are entering for the first time.
      Alternatively you could visit another school and 'notice' these things as
      a way of helping you think about your own school environment.

⇨   Make an effort to notice every aspect of the environment.
      Sometimes it's helpful to think about each sense in turn: what do you
      see, hear, smell, and touch, and taste?
      What are the displays like, as you enter? Is the entrance bright or dim?
      What do the people look like? Do they look happy, or harassed?
      Is it quiet, is there shouting or a hubbub of noise, do the doors squeak?
      Can you smell what lunch will be or the stale smell of yesterday's lunch?
      Is there a Visitors' Book or a touch screen?
      How many doors do you have to negotiate and if you go into the
      staff room, do the cups make a coffee look inviting?

The culture has an impact on the environment but the reverse is also true. If the environment is pleasant, appropriate, safe, and fit for purpose, then people are not only more likely to feel valued but they will probably find it easier to behave in ways that reflect the culture of the setting. If you're thinking this seems shallow, just try to remember the last time you went to an unfamiliar setting and struggled to park your car, or had an arduous journey on public transport, arrived at the place and couldn't get in or attract the receptionist's attention, and eventually were shown into a cold dark room to wait. For all but the very resilient this would have an impact on our mood. We might become less likely to be accommodating. Hopefully, our maturity and professionalism would get us beyond these minor details, but the physical environment truly has impact on us and the way we behave.

A classroom is a place of learning, but for pupils experiencing trouble it also needs to be a place where they can feel nurtured. This is true for pupils who are young but also for those older pupils, the teenagers, whose bodies have matured but who emotionally may have experienced a lag in development because of traumas suffered, lack of opportunity and nurture, the impact of poor attachments or any one of a number of idiopathic causes. Many pupils find noise and busyness difficult to handle. If there is a lot going on, then there will be a higher degree of unpredictability, which other pupils may find equally hard. However, a busy environment can be excellent for learning, so we need to think about how to create some more peaceful micro-environments as escape routes.

Some pupils may function best when they are positioned near a window or the door, or the teacher's desk. Some may work best when they have a particular person next to them. Teachers know that there is a whole range of things that can be done within a classroom to make it better suited to an individual or group of individuals, and of course it's what is routinely done for some children with identified educational needs. Reducing noise can be tough but if you know beforehand that a particular lesson may be noisy then the pupil can be prepared. One of the other big differences I notice on visiting many different primary and secondary schools is the colour, interest and warmth that is often evident in the former, but glaringly absent from the latter. Here again the child or young person whose social or emotional maturity is behind that of his peers may be disadvantaged further by the environment.

Sometimes when I talk to school staff about changing environments they think it may take a lot of effort and be costly - which, admittedly, it may - though it may be preferable to carrying on with an environment that frequently causes issues. But re-arranging the furniture to create a quieter area, or simply investing in a rug or a bean bag may provide a micro-environment either in the classroom or in an inclusion or behaviour unit that some pupils will find more nurturing. And that will usually have a positive impact on the individual's sense of safety and security and therefore on their behaviour.

Now let's think a bit about how we may seek out different or particular environments depending upon our mood or emotional state.

Many of us will seek out comfort if we're not well or feeling upset. We may want to go home, because often that's where we feel safe and secure: we put on our pyjamas or cosy clothes, perhaps find some comfort food or favourite music. We'd probably call a family member, partner or friend if we needed to feel comforted by another person. We seek out all the things we associate with feeling safe and secure and comforted.

Within school settings, such micro-environments can be created which will help children or young people feel safe and secure when they have a need to feel comforted. It's relatively easy to have a room that can be set aside for that purpose, though I accept the constraints of physical environments may mean a whole room is a commitment too far. But many schools have rooms that children will be removed to, so it is often just a matter of reframing how the room is used.

I sometimes hear the objection that if a child is being removed there is a need for punishment of some sort, and to have a room that is nurturing makes this harder. However, I maintain that if a child is removed from class, there needs to be a shared understanding of why. This will usually only emerge when the situation is restored to calm. Many children and young people need space to calm down, so, if they get into a state of distress, then a room they have come to associate with comfort will, over time, help the calming process. The way this is used needs to be monitored, but a carefully constructed environment can speed up the process of actually getting a child back into the classroom where they can continue learning.

Unless the child or young person has a key adult, having a staff member that children feel safe with can present more difficulty if they have other responsibilities, and in these instances using attachment objects may help. Following on from the work of Louise Bombèr (2007, 2011, 2016) and others, many schools have made excellent use of so-called 'attachment objects' to help children feel more secure within the school environment. We all build up associations with objects. An attachment object is something tangible, often a cuddly toy, blanket, or cloth but can be almost anything that becomes very important to a young child to the extent that being separated from it causes distress. Children appreciate objects which can make them feel secure by association to the person who best soothes and comforts them - the bedtime toy is a good example. When children have experienced difficulties with attachment, having an object they associate with the person they have or are developing an attachment to can help them feel secure when that particular person is not present. Some insecure pupils, even older ones, may need a tangible reminder of this person, and bringing the object into school may help. Particular objects within the school environment can also be used when helping pupils learn to manage their emotions. Associating an object with a feeling of calm may help them recognise that state, or even re-find it.

Maisie was in Year 4 and for several days had come to school wearing a really long scarf which she had tripped over on a couple of occasions. Staff suggested she tried a smaller scarf that would be less likely to make her trip. But she persisted in coming with the same long dark blue velvet scarf. Her class teacher made a point of meeting Maisie's gran who regularly picked her up, and asked about the scarf. Gran too had tried to persuade Maisie to swap scarves but this scarf was her mother's, and her mother, who was in the armed services, was away on a tour of duty. Her Gran explained that not only did Maisie wear the scarf to school but took it to bed as well, saying that it smelled of her mum.

Language

Communication is vital within school settings, as it is in all aspects of life, and our choice of language is one of the key ways in which we communicate with each other and everyone else in the setting. It is also one of the ways in which we communicate the culture of the school. As with our environment, language impacts the culture and vice versa. Many of us will have had the experience of feeling really positive at the beginning of the day, then having one particular interaction and our mood plummeting. We have all probably had the reverse, where we've not been on top form, and been really cheered up by a simple interaction with a colleague. What's happening here? And how can we make it work to support us and the other adults and children in our schools?

Before we begin to concentrate on how important positive language is for the children and young people we work with, we need to remember that it is of course important for all of us. In a culture of care there is simply no place for hurtful, negative, sarcastic or belittling comments. I acknowledge that sometimes such comments are made by people who are needy in some way themselves, and we all have our moments; but, I think we'd all acknowledge that it is hypocritical if we have something about valuing everyone in our school mission statement only to have staff speaking to each other in a derogatory and disrespectful way. Even if hard things need to be said, it can be done in a respectful way. If a reprimand is needed, or someone needs holding to account, then this needs to be done in a respectful way, not in front of others and not with a raised voice.

Rose was new to the team of assistants in a college Foundation Studies Department and on leaving a session with very experienced lecturer was surprised to be called back into the classroom. He said he had been 'disgusted' that someone could come into his classroom and not introduce themselves before working with a student. Several students were still present in the classroom, and Rose felt humiliated and belittled by the exchange to an extent that I found her in tears later.

Maybe she had made a mistake. Maybe she did not have enough time, confidence or initiative to go to the front of the class at the beginning before she went to work with her appointed student. But this could have been dealt with by the lecturer simply asking to have a word with her at the end of the session and waiting till students left the room, before simply explaining that the protocol for a new assistant was to introduce themselves to the lecturer before working with the student. The outcome would have been far better for everyone if there had been respect.

Just as when we deal with children, we need to keep our focus on the behaviour, the action (or inaction), not on the person. If the language that is used in the staff room, with parents or visitors and in meetings within the school, is courteous and respectful, it will be much more natural for this to be cascaded to all interactions with children and young people.

When training to be a teacher I remember a discussion about the need for positive language. Having previously worked in a variety of other care settings it seemed obvious, yet it can be hard sometimes to keep language positive while also delivering curriculum, supporting individuals and giving frameworks for behaviour. Language is rooted in culture, and English is a language with lots of words. We don't always talk very directly: we tend to speak in a very polite way, using 'please' and 'thank you', perhaps more than in other languages. Teaching English to foreign language students, they will sometimes ask why we use so many words. One Russian student asked me, why not just say *"Pass the salt"* instead of *"Oh excuse me, would you mind passing the salt when you can, thanks"*. A lot of words, but it is often the way we do things. Yet even with a polite language, that is rich and varied, often with many different words having similar meanings, it still can be hard to ensure our language is positive.

Positive language involves making a choice, firstly about what to comment on, choosing the one thing that you can be positive about, then using positive rather than negative words. It's the difference between saying *"Michael, can you start on the next question now"* and *"Michael can you stop talking."*. The desired outcome is for Michael to do his work, but one is inherently a negative statement while the other is a positive call to a specific action. In the case study above with the assistant Rose it would have been easy for the lecturer to say, *"Thanks for working with Edward, you seem to have developed a great rapport with him. But could I suggest that next time you go to a new class with him that you take a moment to introduce yourself to whoever is teaching the class? Thanks, that would be helpful".* Same outcome, but a call to action given in a positive context instead of something that was critical and humiliating. Whenever you are going to say negative words like '*stop*', '*don't*' or '*no*', pause for a moment, because they can all be reframed in positive sentences.

But there is a lot more to positive language than just not saying negatives. It involves praise, and choosing to comment on the achievements not the failures, on the times things went the right way, not when things went wrong. Using language that is not only respectful but kind, where effort is noted and compliments flow freely. It's the difference between saying,

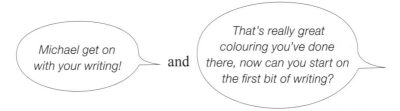

Both include a request or instruction but one takes the opportunity to praise first. As a child (or adult) which would make you most likely to follow the request?

Communicating value

There is a huge amount of communication within a classroom, so there are a lot of opportunities to use positive language. As staff we need to give directions, instructions, comment on behaviour, remind people of expectations, ask questions and give corrections. When communicating with children and young people, we all know that it is important to speak clearly and directly and not use sarcasm, belittle, or openly criticise individuals in front of others. That's simply showing respect and valuing individuals. But it doesn't mean that inappropriate behaviour can't be challenged.

However, when we are dealing with the children and young people who are troubled and may exhibit challenging behaviour, it's very easy to slip into a 'mood' of negativity which of course can be transmitted to the student and make them feel that no-one really expects them to be different: they are the trouble-maker, the one who always gets it wrong. We might all too easily slip into using the kind of comments below. But what are they really communicating to the child or young person?

Very understandable, and it's what we might be thinking: but what do all these phrases say to the child? That *they* are a problem (and not their behaviour): but there is also the message that they will probably *continue* to be a problem. Such comments somehow give a message that they probably won't be able to change.

Words are powerful: many of us probably still remember things that were said to us in school, in fact they may have had an impact upon us for years. But language can also be a great force for good, giving a positive message about the inherent value of the individual and demonstrating our respect. That doesn't mean that language is always rosy - sometimes tough things need saying, but even then our comments can be uttered with kindness. Language which can suggest positive outcomes can be very effective: the examples above could be so different. What might be communicated to the child or young person by these comments?

Some people may think attention to language is pedantic and unnecessary, but we have probably all had experiences where words have hurt or wounded us. Children and young people who are developing their sense of self need lots of positives, pupils who are vulnerable or troubled especially so. We probably all enjoy a positive comment if it sounds sincere. Although some children or young people may struggle with overt praise, many will enjoy casual or informal positive comments. Most adults in school are brilliant at doing this and really using language positively. The difficulty sometimes comes specifically with the children whose behaviour is a challenge: it's hard sometimes even for a consummate professional to keep on being positive when each day feels like a battle. But it is important to keep challenging ourselves to find the right language, or the child will simply feel that they are no good, which is probably what they thought anyway.

The language we use is important, but we all know that language is not just about the words we speak but the way we say them and what our gestures and body language convey at the same time. Emphasising or stressing different words can give a different slant to the meaning.

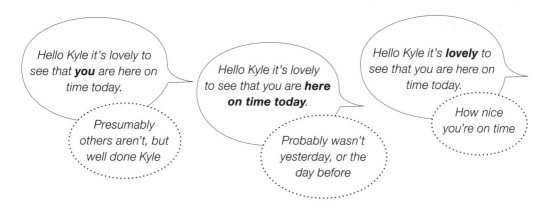

This last variant can be said in all sorts of other ways to convey yet more entirely different meanings. Adding a roll of the eyes to a colleague would rob it of any positivity, and many of us will have been given a compliment at some point where we get the message that it's not sincere from the speaker's facial movements. Some children and young people who have experienced difficult relationships at home may be very skilled at reading gestures. They will be interpreting words and tone of voice and facial expressions while they are being spoken to. Correction if needed should be given with body language that isn't aggressive or intimidating. Many children and young people will find interactions such as reprimands difficult and may appear not to be paying attention. Some will find direct eye contact hard and comments like *"Look at me when I am talking to you"* are likely to inflame an already tense situation further. If we ask them direct questions, they may not reply, or they may deny what everyone knows has just happened. As staff, we need to interpret their communication as reflecting their emotional needs at that moment - they are uncomfortable, they feel ashamed, they feel angry, they are stressed about the consequences - and adjust our ways of communicating with them to at least acknowledge what they are telling us through their behaviour.

Sometimes even when we aware of the particular difficulties of a child or young person, their behaviour warrants particular sanctions. Regrettably, these are often a one-size-fits-all, but where we can differentiate is with the language we use to challenge the behaviour. For all children it should be positive, respectful and kind, but within that framework it can be adjusted to meet the differing needs of individual children and young people whilst still conveying the embedded culture of the setting.

IN SUMMARY

➡ The culture, environment and language of school all contribute to the context in which learning takes place. It is easy to be thrown when the context is not what we expect.

➡ The context of school can remain alien for a lot of children and young people who are troubled. It is vital for these individuals that the context is one of care. A school that has at its core a culture of care will be a good place to work, and to visit. It will be a place where learning will be enhanced for everyone, where challenges are met with consistency and kindness, where every individual feels valued and respected and where there is a sense of security and safety, even for the most vulnerable.

MAIN POINTS

✓ A culture that is caring, that values each individual, shows respect and kindness, is tolerant, challenging, open and transparent, will create a supportive context for learning.

✓ Creating environments in the classroom or elsewhere that allow nurture and make it easy to accommodate differences will help children and young people feel safe, secure and nurtured.

✓ Positive language, in words and in gesture, is essential to communicate the values of the culture of care and ensure that children and young people who are not ready to learn have a context in which they can *become* ready to learn.

CHAPTER 3

The spectrum of trouble

Let's start to look at the kinds of difficulties and traumas the children and young people in our classrooms may have experienced. Many people reading this will be aware of some of the factors, but it's important to explore the range or *spectrum* of troubles and challenges that far too many have encountered. From the severe and sadly often long lasting trauma of a child who may be abused, to the more transient and less severe issues and worries that others may experience, they will all have an impact upon our pupils' readiness to learn. Some may have built up a degree of emotional or supportive 'capital' which may lessen the impact of the trouble, but still their readiness to learn can be affected. The better we understand the impact, the more we will be in a position to help them.

If we could see their 'baggage', if children carried their emotions like their back packs, I wonder what we'd see.

As I stand in the playground and see the children come through the gates I might notice that Tanya's head is down, she's tired, I suspect her older brother has been having more ferocious arguments with his father, that have so often led to violence. Ruth, a young mum with severe mental health problems is trying her best to care for her two young ones but as they trail far behind her I can see from her eyes that she is not really 'present' - at least as twins the children have each other. Franklyn is kicking a stone along as he shouts repeatedly, trying to get his mother's attention, but she is chatting to someone on the phone and just turns to shoot him angry glances. Antonio is with his grandmother, which probably means his mother is having another round of chemotherapy; and neither of the Samatar children are present so that will mean a call to the social worker as they only remain in their home, acknowledged to be neglected, with an aggressive mother who deals with her own issues by misusing a wide variety of substances, on condition that they attend school each day and clubs at the weekend.

Of course there are also the children who come through the gate laughing with siblings and friends, sharing a joke with a mum or dad as their attentive parents check they've remembered everything and give them a hug or kiss, even wait for a last wave as the child moves into the line.

REFLECTIVE ACTIVITY

⇨ Think about a day when you have some personal issues and think what would help you at the start of the day as you go into school, and what would make it worse.

⇨ Then focus for a moment on two children from your class or school with contrasting home lives.

⇨ Then think about the start to the school day in your setting.

⇨ Does it work equally well for both?

⇨ Could it be changed easily to make it more nurturing?
Perhaps remember the things that have sometimes helped you?

The nature and spectrum of 'trouble'

Schools are all different. Each classroom is a little different to the next, and of course our individual pupils are all unique. But we can be pretty certain that in most classrooms there will be children and young people who could aptly be described as 'troubled'. At the severe end of the spectrum, there will be some children who have experienced trauma on a repeated basis, possibly for most of their lives. Others will have suffered what many of us would now recognise as *attachment difficulties* (Geddes 2006), through having had no secure, consistent attachments in their early life. There may be some children who have been removed from their parents and taken into care. The hope would be that this would signal a beginning to the healing process, but what we know is that their trauma often continues, involving foster placement moves, separation from siblings and the often essential, but none the less traumatic, contact with parents or other family members. There may be the trauma of court involvement and tragically, some children are blamed by other family members for 'causing' these events.

But while we know that children taken into public care account for a tiny half of one per cent of the school population, we also know they are not the only children who are 'troubled'. Through the case studies and commentary in this chapter, I'm going to explore what I think of as the 'spectrum of trouble'.

The word spectrum is defined by The Oxford English Dictionary (2016) as
'used to classify something in terms of its position on a scale between two extreme points'

On any given day in any classroom there will be children and young people who are on the spectrum of trouble, regularly or occasionally. As I show in the diagram overleaf, some will be coping with relatively minor difficulties, but these still may be sufficient to upset the pupil for a time, and make formal learning difficult. Also, any 'event' will be experienced differently by different individuals because of their *particular circumstances*, and because of their *individual responses* to those circumstances. The level of resilience they have or don't have, the capital of support and strength they have or haven't developed before (or during) the experience of trouble, will all have bearing on what happens.

THE SPECTRUM OF TROUBLE

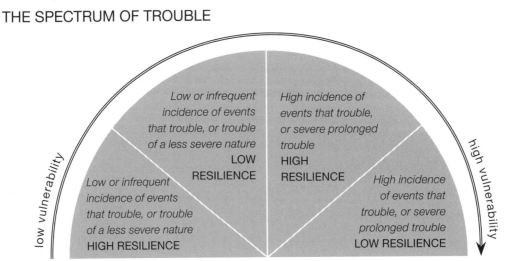

In this chapter I'll look at some specific case studies so we can consider the extent and variety of trouble that children and young people experience: for some, short lived, but for others involving considerable time before they would reliably be in a social and emotional state that meant they were ready to learn. And, importantly, I'll note en route the factors that can create a 'cushion' of resilience, which may have a mitigating effect on the way the experience of trouble impacts a pupil's life, development and learning.

Severe or significant trouble BEREAVEMENT

I'm going to start with an account that highlights the impact of the significant trouble which is a major loss or bereavement. Sadly many children suffer loss, perhaps of distant relatives, friends or pets, and this may well be very upsetting. But loss of a close family member or one to whom they had significant attachment may have a devastating, even life changing impact, often the case when a parent dies. While we can never say that one type of bereavement is more or less significant than another, and certainly not dictate an individual's response to profound grief and loss, we can probably see that there is a difference between the two case studies below, in the level of support each pupil has received.

Gemma was six when her mother Karen was diagnosed with breast cancer, and seven when Karen died. Gemma's father was given time off from work to care for his wife for the last six months. Prior to that when her mother was undergoing chemotherapy or at other times of difficulty, Gemma's grandparents came to stay and took her to school and did much of the running of the home. In fact they moved nearer to the family so they could continue supporting their daughter's family after her death. The family had a good relationship with the village school that Gemma attended, and kept in close contact so they too could support her.

The whole family were involved with a support group and in as gentle and appropriate way as they could manage, Gemma was told that her mother was going to die and was able to spend some good times with her. Gemma's Mum and grandmother worked on a photograph album and 'keepsake' box for Gemma.

Gemma went to the cremation and even took part in the private family scattering of the ashes. Several adults from the school and a couple of other children, who with their families were close to Gemma and her family, also attended the service.

Sundeep was 12 when his mother was in a fatal car crash. His father was also in the car and suffered a serious head injury and was hospitalised for several months. Sundeep had an older brother of 15. No other family members lived in this country and efforts to trace family members elsewhere proved difficult. Sundeep was taken into care, initially placed with his brother in an emergency placement but moved to separate placements when his brother kept absconding and the foster carers felt they couldn't manage either the behaviour or the frequent trips to hospital and the fairly lengthy daily journey to school.

Sundeep's brother, who had his 16th birthday a few weeks later, elected to move into supported lodgings. Sundeep moved to three different foster placements but his behaviour continued to challenge both at school, where he experienced a number of exclusions, and in the foster care placements. He was living in a residential children's home some distance *from his home when his father died.   There had still been no success in tracing family members who could care for Sundeep.*

Every child's experience is unique to them as an individual; a single event like a bereavement, will be different in every case.   Each child is an individual and their response to that event will depend on a wide range of factors, including the support they do or don't receive, as we can see from these two examples.   While we may be able to notice some patterns, the response is individual to that child and we won't always be able to accurately predict what that will be.   What *would* be reasonable to assume however, is that for a time, while Gemma and Sundeep and other bereaved children may be in class, they may not be ready at any level to learn, as so much of their energy, both physical and emotional, will be being used to simply keep going.

Severe or significant trouble ABUSE OR NEGLECT

According to NSPCC (2016) statistics, 57,000 children were identified as needing protection from abuse with an increase in reports of sexual offences against children; and, in England and Wales, an increase in the number of recorded cruelty and neglect offences. But it would seem reasonable to assume that not every case is reported so the numbers of children actually suffering is probably much higher.   The NSPCC also reported an increase in the number of children within the child protection system but estimated that for every child identified as needing protection from abuse another eight might be suffering abuse.   Neglect was a feature of one in six serious case reviews.   Brandon et al (2013) and the Department for Education (2016) reported that there were 70,440 children who were Looked after in March 2016, a continual rise over recent years.   Research by Radford et al (2011) showed that one in five children experienced maltreatment and that one in three of children sexually abused did not tell anyone at the time.

The numbers of suffering children may not be shared out equally among schools of course, with some schools having a much higher proportion of these children than others.

But most of these children will be attending school every day while experiencing extreme distress. It is a disturbing picture.

In addition, as is all too obvious to all of us working in education, regrettably there are children and young people who experience woefully inadequate parenting. Some of these may be known to social care services and may even experience times of being in care, whilst others will not. They will just keep on surviving, often with older siblings taking on a caring role for their younger brothers and sisters. These are the children whose parents simply lack the resources (emotional, financial, or intellectual), to care for their child or children adequately, in a consistent way, or they may struggle with addiction or mental health issues. The parents themselves may have experienced a childhood which was far from good enough. There may be times when meals and clean uniforms are available to these children, times when parents can be nurturing, but there may also be times when their parents can barely look after themselves, let alone a child or children. The impact for some children and young people may be lessened by members of the extended family, but for others there simply may not be an extended family, or one that would be in a position to offer help.

Tyrone was eight when social workers, alerted by the school, visited his house. Tyrone frequently arrived at school late, was smelly and always appeared hungry. The family were known to the social care services: Tyrone's mother had herself been in care, had learning disabilities and had three children younger than Tyrone who also lived with her in the two bedroomed flat. The pattern that had developed was of service involvement which led to improvements in the standard of care as intensive support was given, but then, when the support was withdrawn because things had apparently improved, the level of care diminished once again. Undoubtedly, Tyrone's mother loved her children, but she lacked the capacity to adequately care for them all in a consistent way. When social workers visited, the house was dirty, beds had no bedding, mattresses were soiled, bin bags were piled in the hall and the fridge was empty.

Steph was taken into care following a disclosure at school of serious sexual abuse. She was 13. The picture that emerged following police investigation was one of ongoing sexual abuse by male members of the extended family - who were later imprisoned. It was thought the abuse began when she was about eight. Steph received a lot of support from mental health services but at 15 became pregnant. Until her disclosure, no-one had suspected anything: her attendance at school had been excellent though she was seen as a shy, quiet girl - her parents (usually mother) had always attended parents' evenings and other functions. Her parents had separated and the abuse happened when her mother's new partner moved into the home. Steph had three younger half-brothers.

Anyone who has experienced a relatively normal, loving family life, albeit with limitations, can't really begin to imagine the level of trauma and distress that Tyrone and Steph experienced while turning up at school each day, generally taking part in most of the lessons and playing with peers at break and lunchtimes. Undoubtedly these are children and young people at the extreme end of the troubled spectrum, though certainly in the case of Steph, not a child who was difficult to teach. For a variety of reasons Tyrone and Steph didn't have external support mechanisms that could minimise the impact of the troubling events in their lives (despite social care involvement for Tyrone), so they are examples of pupils experiencing significant trouble with low levels of resilience. There were few buffers for either pupil, between them and what was happening to and around them: in the case of Steph, it seems she internalised the anguish she must have been feeling as there was little change in her behaviour whilst the abuse was happening.

Transient or lower level trouble

But with every spectrum of course there are children who experience trouble to a lesser though still significant extent. The last two children mentioned above have both experienced prolonged trauma, a severe form of what we might think of as trouble, which happened consistently over an extended period. But what we also know is that there are other sorts of trouble or trauma, as shown in the following case studies, that can impact our pupils and students and which may make them either unable to learn or experience difficulty in learning for a period of time.

Chloe is ten - she lives with her mother and she has a severely disabled older brother. Her brother attends a special school each day but in the evenings he is increasingly difficult for his mother to manage. He wets and soils, and as he is now almost adult sized, at age 14, his mother struggles to change him. He is non-verbal, but makes a loud screaming noise when excited or distressed. His mother gets some support but respite care has now been reduced to one day per month and one weekend every three months. Chloe never has friends to her house and her mother recently confessed to Chloe's teacher that she is feeling incredibly depressed and struggling to cope but does not want social service involvement.

Karim is 15; he has an older sister, Aapti, with severe cystic fibrosis, a condition requiring frequent hospitalisation. In addition to his own emotions about his sister's condition, Karim also has to live with his parents' emotions about his sister. Clearly each hospitalisation is increasingly worrying: Aapti's condition is deteriorating and as a family they know they may have to face her premature death. Karim's parents are trying their best to cope with a difficult situation. So is Karim, but he confessed to his English teacher that he finds it increasingly difficult to concentrate on his studies and feels guilty enjoying life.

Tiegan was six and her parents were both in the army. She and her sister were used to moves and used to one or the other parent being away. They also knew families where parents had been posted abroad and been injured or killed. They lived on the base where their father was posted and attended the local school. Their mother was working on a project which involved frequent trips abroad and both Tiegan and her sister were reported by the school to exhibit very challenging behaviour when their mother went away.

Harry *and Stuart were twins in Year 5 in junior school. Their father commuted to London and frequently had to go abroad but was also one of the governors of the school. As a family they were very involved in local village life, attending scouts and Saturday morning football. When their mother and father separated, their father moved to London and they only saw him once a month for the weekend. Their mother said they missed him terribly.*

Jodie *was seven years old. Jodie's parents had split up when she was very small. From being tiny she regularly spent weekends and holidays with her dad. Her mother had lived with three different partners since her dad had left and she had two children by two of her previous partners. Recently she had moved in with another man who had two children of his own. Sometimes there were five children in the home, at other times less. Jodie was now having to share a room with her new step-sister aged nine whenever the step-sister came to stay with her dad (mum's new partner).*

Sukinder *(12) had a sister and brother who were both younger than she was. The family used to live in a large house on the outskirts of the city, but bankruptcy forced them to move to a small rented flat, which in turn necessitated a school move, from an expensive private school to a local city comprehensive. Teachers reported that they were all having difficulty settling into their new school.*

In these instances, children were attending school while trying to deal with complex and sometimes distressing emotions triggered by complicated circumstances. Some were undoubtedly more resilient in the situations they found themselves because of support they received or relationships that may have been protective in some way. Jodie, for example, continued to enjoy weekends with her dad who was never reported to have a new partner, so the complex step-sibling relationships and somewhat chaotic or changeable domestic situation at her mother's home was perhaps countered to a degree by the relative stability she experienced in her relationship with her father.

But, as we shall see, changes in our society mean that there may be more children coping with family change than previously in our classrooms. They may not be suffering extreme trauma, but they may well be preoccupied and using most of their emotional energy worrying about changes which can involve school moves, and possibly moves away from some of the relationships that provided a degree of support for them to cope with the challenges they face.

REFLECTIVE ACTIVITY

⇨ Pick just 2 of the scenarios listed in the case studies above.

⇨ Think about what kind of support could be provided for the pupils you have chosen.

⇨ Then think about your school setting and think how you would identify the pupils or students in need of support and how such support could be incorporated into the day-to-day timetable of the school.

Social change and the spectrum of trouble

In 2013 in the UK there were 114,720 divorces (Office of National Statistics 2013). But almost half of these couples (48%) had at least one child aged under 16 living with them. For some of our pupils, this may not have been their first experience of parental separation. Some of them will experience acute anxiety and a sense of loss and separation from a parent with whom they have a strong attachment. If the process is managed well, then they will hopefully continue to have contact with both parents. If this person is a step-parent, however, this may not happen, since there is no biological tie; but we know that 'attachment' is hard to measure. The pupil themselves may be unaware of the degree of attachment they had with a step-parent until that adult is gone from their life.

Aaron was 13 when his mother left his stepfather. They had been together for five years. Aaron saw his dad during holidays but it was his stepfather who came to school functions and so on. His dad now lived 200 miles away as his mother had moved to be nearer her parents following the break-up of her relationship with Aaron's dad. Following the break-up there was a noticeable decline in the level and quality of his work in school, and he also got involved in a few lunchtime 'squabbles'.

He told a learning mentor sometime later that it was his stepfather who had helped with homework, and who had made sure that he and his step-siblings were ready for school. No formal arrangements had been made for contact, but school became aware that the step-father had moved in with the mother of another boy in the school. Not only had Aaron lost him, a significant figure in his life, but someone he knew had 'gained' both him and his children, Aaron's step-siblings.

A survey by ICM (The Guardian 2008) highlighted concern about the current low numbers of male teachers in primary schools. Of the 800 men questioned, 35% said that having a male teacher in primary school had challenged them to work harder and 50% said they would be more likely to approach a male teacher about bullying. In part, that concern has come about because of the broader concern about young children, perhaps especially boys, growing up without positive male role models. Sadly we have systems in place in our society which are meant to provide a safety net and a means to ensure at least financial support for children; yet they may actually mitigate against a child maintaining an ongoing relationship with the father. The Child Support Agency will simply reduce payments made by a father to a mother if the child stays over with the father. For some women separated from the children's father, that may be a good reason to argue against contact or prevent overnight contact.

It is also hard to understand why there is still no presumption of shared residency. Many have argued that children need routine and security, but in my experience of working with children and young people, unless there is a compelling reason to the contrary, children should have time with both parents and separation, or uncertainty about when they will see a parent they have an attachment to, may be more damaging than not always having a solid routine. Environment does play an important part in security for a child: but relationships are even more pivotal. Inconvenience should never be a reason why an important relationship is not nurtured.

> *Mia (six) was noticed to be especially and uncharacteristically quiet for several days. The next day it was the birthday of one of the others in her class, and Mia just burst into tears. When she was sitting with the assistant, Kirsty, outside class, Mia told Kirsty how she was due to go to see her Dad and brother at the weekend (as was usual) but it was her Mum's birthday, and she was worried she wouldn't be able to go. But she didn't want to miss her Mum's birthday either.*

Some children will worry about things and get emotional about things that may not seem very big, but they will be enough to distract some children. Maybe her mother had it all under control and had discussed with her ex - Mia's Dad - but maybe not.

Even as adults, managing some relationships can be difficult, and most parents with children that I know who are not living with their child's father would readily admit that despite their best effort as humans they have messed things up at times and not anticipated things which have been issues for the child, or foreseen the impact these issues may actually have had.

Economic stress and poverty

Although it has been reported (2015 BBC) that there has been a decrease in the number of people unemployed (with a jobless rate of 6% - the lowest in six years, at the time of writing), many of us will be aware of someone who has either lost their job or moved their place of work in the hope of escaping redundancy. For those who are in work, we read of the rise in zero hours contracts which afford little security or protection to workers - a day off often means no pay, and a few days off may mean the job is lost. Not an easy position to be in for parents who may face having to work around their child being excluded, or on a reduced timetable. During the last year we have seen reports of payday lenders, changes to the benefits system and tax credit system, and a sizable reduction of funding to both local governments and many of the other services that support children and families. The Child Poverty Action group (2015) estimate that there are 3.9 million children living in poverty in the UK. That's about nine in a class of 30. In addition to the economic impact that having little money brings, poverty brings many other consequences for health, education and the community as a whole (CPAG 2013). Children from poorer backgrounds lag behind at all stages of education.*

Naturally, poverty or economic pressure causes worry and uncertainty as well as financial constraints. Not all of us as adults are able to manage anxiety so effectively that it does not spill over into or have some impact on our families. A lot of children will be going to school each day with an awareness that their parents are not quite how they usually are: they may not know or understand the reasons why, but they will probably 'feel' the difference. This is in addition of course to perhaps experiencing the impact of poverty: feeling hungry, not sleeping because they feel cold, perhaps feeling different from peers without perhaps knowing why.

Teaching occurs within a context of the whole society. Statistics may give us a glimpse of current trends our pupils are having to cope with, but they won't know these - they just know what's happening to them.

Self-image and self-esteem

We know that there are a huge number of children who experience problems with self-esteem. Again the 'cause' of this will vary and it may or may not be apparent what the underlying issue may be. To give one example: estimates suggest 28% of children

---

* By the age of three, poorer children are estimated to be, on average, nine months behind children from more wealthy backgrounds. According to Department for Education statistics, by the end of primary school, pupils receiving free school meals are estimated to be almost three terms behind their more affluent peers. By 14, this gap grows to over five terms. By 16, children receiving free school meals achieve 1.7 grades lower at GCSE

between the ages of two and 15 are overweight or obese (Dept. of Health 2015). That is a lot of children who may go to school each day feeling anxious about comments others may make, dreading PE lessons or maybe dreading lunchtimes where there may be talk of food, or insults, or perhaps a very restricted meal.

Many children suffer from low self-esteem and lack of confidence for other reasons, but gathering accurate statistics may be difficult because of course it is something that many of our pupils will try to hide. What we do know is that self-harm is increasing: 2014 figures from *Self Harm UK* suggest a 70% increase in young people between ten and 16 going to Accident and Emergency units because of self-harm related issues. Self-harm is the extreme end of the scale and there will be very many more children and young people who experience issues with their self-image, feeling unattractive, different from others, not as clever or socially able as others, not liked by their peers or experiencing bullying which can be serious and kept hidden until real damage may have been done.

We can see from this section that while we might have 30 children or young people sitting in rows in our classroom, possibly even of broadly similar ability, their experiences (the things which may make them behave very differently from their classroom neighbour) will be unique to them and may well be completely concealed. We can read the paper and keep abreast of changes in our society that are likely to impact the cohort of pupils or students we know, but that's a far cry from understanding what they may be experiencing.

REFLECTIVE ACTIVITY

⇨ Think about a group of pupils or students you have regular contact with and identify those who you know often present as a 'challenge'.

⇨ How much do you know about their situation outside school, or in school in relation to their peers?

Some of the 'troubles' that I've just highlighted may be much more transient in nature than the ones I described earlier in the chapter. Children can often adjust well to parental separation or drops in family income, particularly when they are given support. There will always be some children who struggle with self-esteem for a variety of reasons and many individual schools are skilled at dealing with these children in supportive ways. What we know of children, indeed humans, is that they are adaptable, and generally resilient. On the whole, our pupils cope with all sorts of difficulties. But it can still mean they come to school feeling distressed at least on some occasions, at least for a time.

The way that distress manifests itself of course varies too, but what does not vary is that the children are aware of distress and trouble - they 'feel' it. They live through times of worry and fear and emotional difficulty and some will feel well supported, but not all. They may have adults around who have the capacity and skills to support and help them in an appropriate way. But they may not. Some have to deal with these issues pretty much on their own.

We know something of the impact of prolonged or repeated trauma on children. The Office for National Statistics quoted on the NHS website (2014) reported that 10% of children and young people in Great Britain suffer from a recognisable mental disorder with 4% suffering from an emotional disorder such as anxiety or depression. Children and young people will be stressed by all sorts of things like exams and pressure to perform well but also from experiences as I've been describing; parental break-ups, illness, peer pressure, bullying, to list just a few. Such stress may have an impact on their education as well as their wellbeing.

A recent piece of research - *Family Stressors and Children's Outcomes* (Jones et al 2013) - showed that some stressful events could have an enduring effect on educational outcomes and wellbeing. Some events, for example domestic abuse, being placed in care, or victimisation or abuse outside of the home were associated with lower Key Stage 3 attainment and poorer wellbeing among teenagers, regardless of *when* in the young people's lives these events had occurred. However, other events, such as death, serious illness in the family or arrest of a family member had an impact on wellbeing, but not on educational attainment.

The events that seem to cause the greatest damage educationally are those where the difficulties *encountered* and the *lack of protective factors available* to them place the children or young people at the severe end of the spectrum of trouble, in ways that impact the core of their lives, their home, their personal safety, their worth. These will be the children who may be sitting in class but are unlikely to be able to learn, possibly for prolonged periods. But in addition to these children, there will be many others who are experiencing less severe trauma, perhaps also trouble of a more transient nature: but they too, for a time, may be unable to learn.

Perhaps most revealing was that stressful events such as parental divorce, parental arguing or not seeing family members or siblings as much as usual were associated with lower educational attainment or worse wellbeing *but,* only when this occurred when the child was over the age of seven. In the middle years of childhood they start to think about the future, understand more about their place in the world, learn better ways to describe their feelings and start to show more concern for others. A younger child is perhaps more rooted in the present: but a child of seven or older is better able to place things in a context, so perhaps has an understanding that this separation, divorce, lack of contact and so on will continue. Perhaps at a simple level they are less able to be distracted because they 'know' what they will be missing, because they have experienced something different.

Children and young people who are troubled are usually attending school: teachers like ourselves know them and teach them every day. Sometimes we may be aware of some of the difficulties they are experiencing, but not always. Often there will be some noticeable change in their behaviour, but again, not always, and perhaps it's this unpredictability that makes understanding what's happening so hard.

IN SUMMARY

So I've given you a brief overview of what I think of as the 'spectrum of trouble' that children encounter, leaving them more or less vulnerable at different times. In each of our classrooms of course there are also adults, equally experiencing different kinds of troubles. There are likely to be some key differences in the ways we, as adults, respond to emotional turmoil.

▶   In the next chapter I'll look at some of the ways that as adults we can manage our own emotions, and then how we can teach some of the strategies we use effectively ourselves to the children and young people we work with.

MAIN POINTS

✓   Children and young people may experience a 'spectrum of trouble' during their school years.

✓   These may be of a short or long term nature, but all or any of them may affect readiness to learn.

✓   Some pupils may be supported through difficult times by family, friends or statutory or voluntary agencies, and have a degree of resilience. Others may not have access to much support or much resilience, leaving them highly vulnerable.

CHAPTER 4

Managing our own emotions

In the last chapter I looked at the 'spectrum of trouble' which our pupils and students may be experiencing or have experienced. School staff can also sometimes feel stressed or anxious for a variety of reasons. We adults experience numerous difficulties in our day-to-day lives that cause us to respond emotionally. Even if these difficulties don't have direct impact on our development or educational attainment as they might for a child or young person, they can still present challenges to our capacity to remain professional in our various roles.

My daughter who was travelling literally on the other side of the world, called me by surprise one afternoon at 2am her time. She was locked out of her house, couldn't reach any of her friends and had also injured her arm which was bleeding 'quite a bit' in her words. To make matters worse, her phone battery was about to run out - which it did. At that point I had no way of contacting her and simply had to wait for another phone call from either her or someone else to tell me that she was safe and well, or at least that was what I was hoping for. In fact a phone call came about four hours later to inform us that she had been taken to hospital and had stitches in her arm but by then was safely back home with the friends she shared the house with, who did a great job of looking after her and reassuring me.

As you can imagine, during the few intervening hours remaining focused and professional was a 'bit of a challenge' for me. Things happen. We respond to events with emotion; but we manage them even when it's a challenge, so as to maintain our functionality and professionalism - more or less, better at times than at others, and if it is a serious issue we sometimes need to step out of our professional role for a while, for example following a bereavement.

We live with our emotions. We have no choice: they are an essential part of what makes us human. They bring us our happiest moments and our saddest: to live a life without emotions would be a half-life, little more than being a robot, an automaton. On the other hand, to live our whole life overwhelmed by emotion would be equally untenable. So as adults we develop ways of 'managing' or dealing with our emotions with strategies that for most adults will usually be effective, unless the situation is extreme.

In the school context, being upset or anxious about something can definitely have an impact on the way we work. Naturally we all do certain things to minimise any impact on the pupils we teach or the roles we fulfil, and it's worth reflecting on what these are.

So before I go on to examine *how* we manage our emotions and *why* that process is important for the children and young people we work with, please spend a few moments thinking about the following questions.

REFLECTIVE ACTIVITY

⇨ Think back to an occasion when you arrived at school feeling very upset or anxious about something. It works best to think of a real scenario if you can.

⇨ Then label or name the different emotions you felt - it might be just one, sadness, for example, or several, sad, (because someone is very ill), frustrated (maybe medical staff not appearing to do things quickly enough) and perhaps anger (some family members not responding the way you thought they should).

⇨ What did you do to ensure you could continue to be an effective team member that day? Try to be as specific as possible.
Don't just say *"I talked to someone"*. Be specific: what did you tell them? What did they say? How did it help?

In this chapter I'll be looking at emotions and what we mean by genuinely 'managing' them - neither suppressing nor constantly expressing feelings (*see below*), but dealing with them in a way that's healthy for us, and enables us to continue to be effective practitioners offering support to the children, young people and adults we work with each day (even when sometimes it's working with them that's causing us to respond emotionally!).

If we as adults are able to cope well with our emotional life, and understand the process and strategies we use to do so, we'll be better able to help our pupils on the troubled spectrum learn how to deal with what *they* experience (although the situations they are in may be more 'extreme' than things we've experienced). The better we can do that, the more able we'll be to help them get to a position where they are really ready to learn.

What are emotions?

The word emotion usually refers to a mental state with accompanying physical sensations that arises spontaneously, in response to external or internal stimuli. Adrenaline, for example, is released in response to fear, often known as the 'fight, flight or freeze' response, which causes our hearts to beat rapidly, pupils to dilate, body to sweat, skin to become pale and breathing to become more rapid - to mention just a few of the physical effects. The stimulus happens, in this case the frightening thing, and our body responds, creating a whole range of physical sensations and feelings which we give an emotional label to in our minds. We don't usually make a *conscious* decision about how we feel; we simply respond to a stimulus by feeling particular sensations, both physical and emotional. If we're doing something we enjoy, we're likely to feel a positive emotion, happiness or contentment: if we're about to go on holiday we may feel excited or possibly nervous. If we're facing a test, or possible redundancy, we may feel anxious, or if someone hasn't done something we thought they were going to do we may feel angry.

Our feelings or emotions are usually responses to what is happening. On most occasions we know or understand exactly why we are experiencing a particular emotion - a feeling of sadness on hearing that a close friend or family member is very ill, disappointed when an event we've looked forward to is cancelled, or surprise and excitement if we win something. But on other occasions, our emotions may not be so clear: we might feel sad or 'low' without knowing why, for example. In addition, we can experience a whole range of emotions in response to single events: for example the loss of a loved one can cause grief and sorrow but often anger, possibly relief if they'd been suffering; possibly guilt; a promotion may trigger happiness and pride, but maybe apprehension too about the new challenges, and anxiety about the way colleagues may respond in future. So there can be a mixed emotional response to these single events and if they are significant or traumatic, like bereavement, our feelings can last for a very long time.

So -
  i   emotions are a response to events, rather than
       something we choose
  ii   emotions are usually beyond our conscious control
       (though how we deal with them may not be)
and
  iii we may experience several different emotions in response to a
       single event and these may last for a long time if the event is
       significant or traumatic.

It's important that we're clear about these key things before we move on to consider the ways in which we deal with emotions.

As adults we have usually learned how to express our feelings in an appropriate and reasonably measured way. But that hasn't always been the case - we weren't born with such coping strategies, we had to learn them as we grew up. As with other aspects of learning, such learning will vary from person to person depending on the opportunities we've been given to learn, and whether or not we were able and ready to learn.

A friend visited our home the other day, with her two small children aged three and six. When it was time to go the children were enjoying playing with a toy kitchen and had set up a shop and restaurant. The six year old pulled a bit of a face and asked if she had to stop, but complied almost immediately. This was not the case with the three year old, who began to whine and then cry, and continued to cry till she was carried to the car by her mother.

When upset, teenagers may shout and storm, go quiet and look at their feet or simply exit the situation, which was what happened not long back when I witnessed one young man being told he was excluded (which he felt was very unfair). An adult friend was recently extremely disappointed when she realised she hadn't managed to get a job she really wanted. She was obviously upset but handled this by simply requesting a meet-up with a mate and having a good old 'offload' over coffee and cake before being able to put it behind her.

We all get upset. It's part of life. It's tough to stop doing something we enjoy: it's hard when things happen that we think are unfair: and disappointment is almost always tough to handle. But most of us learn to manage these feelings in ways that are more appropriate than the example of the three year old above and possibly the teenager. We do so because we've learned how to. We know that good times have to stop, that there are ways of tackling unfair situations without storming out and we develop a range of ways that help us deal with things like disappointment. That's because we've developed an understanding of 'life'. By the time we are adult we know that most situations can be resolved, or we can learn to live with them. The emotions we feel are generally not unusual because we've often experienced them before, and we may have tried out different ways of dealing with them, although of course we can still encounter a 'new' situation, like the first major relationship break-up or perhaps a bereavement. Most of us have worked out effective strategies for different 'emotional' situations. We've also probably learned that the response we get should we have a tantrum, shout loudly or become abusive is not likely to be a positive one. So if we do want to yell, we might choose to do it elsewhere.

Most of us will have had times of being upset over something and reacting much like the three year old above; many of us will even remember the specific incidents, whatever age we were at the time! Please spend a few moments thinking about who helped you learn alternative ways of behaving when you felt these emotions, how they did that and what strategies they used.

REFLECTIVE ACTIVITY

⇨   Think back to an occasion (or several) when you were very upset over something.

⇨   Try to remember the emotions you felt and name these.

⇨   What did others DO or SAY to help you cope?

⇨   What did you learn from these experiences?

I imagine many people will have come up with things like being hugged if you cried, chastised if you shouted or threw things, but also perhaps adults saying that the feelings would pass, and, as you got older, maybe suggesting things like a walk to calm down or a mug of hot chocolate!

A friend of mine who grew up in care laughingly told me that she was in her early 20's before she realised that when you were cross with someone you didn't have to shout and scream and slam doors. She may well have been exaggerating a little, but spending a lot of her early childhood with a mother who found it hard to function and her teenage years in children's homes, with other young people who had experienced extreme emotions and not been in environments or relationships where they could learn to manage them, there was undoubtedly some truth in it.

So we know that we experience emotions in response to events and these emotions may be very mixed, and that as adults after a long period of maturity and development with the right support we have probably all learned some ways to deal with them.

Ongoing and reactive emotions

Whilst some emotions arise from the ongoing events in our lives, for example, difficult relationships, illness, worry about a family member or a house move, there are also the legions of 'reactive' emotions we feel every day. When we wake up we may feel dread about a particular lesson or regret that we stayed up way too late watching TV: cross that there is no milk, that the car is low on petrol, or positive rage when someone cuts us up at a junction. All this - and more - has happened before we even step into the staff room, let alone the classroom. These emotions are usually in response to events of the day, things that happen, situations, people, practical difficulties; they may be transient in nature but they can still have an impact - as we all know.

REFLECTIVE ACTIVITY

⇨ Think for a moment about the last time you arrived at work, or walked into your classroom, feeling like a shaken 'snow globe'. Think about -

⇨ What had caused the feelings?

⇨ Was it a single 'thing' or a build-up of several?

⇨ What you did at the time to make sure you could remain professional?

⇨ How was the situation resolved?

These reactive emotions crop up throughout our day and we experience them against the backdrop of our ongoing or background emotional state. In a busy, stimulating environment like school, there will be a lot of emotional stimuli, and we have probably all had times where we have 'overreacted' to a simple, immediate situation because of the background emotion that we're also trying to deal with. Being really angry with our child who is slow to get ready for school when we are actually very worried about a family member's health is a straightforward and easy to recognise example. When we end up arguing with a close friend or partner over something trivial, it's often because we're upset or stressed about things that have happened at work, though it may take us a while to realise this. Many of us might have experienced suddenly feeling close to tears or yelling or getting terse over something like misplacing a piece of paper or not finding a car parking space, but this is usually a 'last straw' of mounting pressure, just one more small thing that's simply too much to cope with given everything else that's happening. It's not that we are unaware of the other situations but we are also getting on with the business of the day, possibly not dealing as well as we might with the 'other' underlying emotions, until something happens that means we just can't keep going and we 'snap' in some way.

> To re-cap:
>
> iv   we experience emotions in response to a stimulus
> v   some are more long lasting than others
> vi   sometimes emotions created by a background situation will
>   have impact on how we respond to current situations

Now we're going to look at how situations from the past, and the emotions we experienced at those times, can also have an impact on how we respond to situations in the present.

The influence of the past

There are many different factors influencing our emotional response to particular situations, and its strength. Our responses can be affected by other emotions, as well as the current situation and our wellbeing (or lack of wellbeing). In addition, personality, family, upbringing and culture will all have bearing. Previous experience of both similar events and the emotion we've experienced previously in such situations will also have an impact.

I was recently in the car with a colleague who was driving and when someone pulled out at a junction in front of us, inconsiderately but not really dangerously. I was surprised by her reaction, which seemed to me quite over the top. It was only as we talked later that I found out she had been involved in a serious car accident when she was a teenager, because someone had pulled out at a junction. Her reaction to the current event was clearly and understandably influenced by her previous experience.

Sometimes of course our response is more related to the emotion we experience, than to any similarity of the event itself.

*Another colleague, **Sophia**, received a phone call at work and became extremely upset. The call was from her adult daughter Fiona, who had recently recovered from a very serious illness. In fact the problem she called about was a minor issue (she had locked herself out), but as my colleague explained, she was so used to receiving distressed phone calls from her daughter when Fiona had been in hospital, and had at that time felt the stress of not being able to 'solve' the problems she'd encountered, that as soon as she had an unexpected phone call from Fiona she instinctively remembered those distressing emotions. It was the emotions she had experienced previously that influenced Sophia's response to the current situation.*

Many of us will have experienced that phenomenon, though may not realise it at the time or connect 'the dots' until later. As humans we're constantly interpreting the stimuli we're faced with at a subconscious level. What we've learned and 'stored' in our subconscious about 'that type of stimulus' will often surface when something similar happens; like Sophia, we go into an autopilot response. Her daughter called and was upset - an experience she had come across before, or so her subconscious thought, and in the past this had led to serious distress for Sophia. So her unconscious immediately 'switched on' what had previously been the 'appropriate' response. In this case of course it wasn't proportionate, and given time, and repeated unalarming experiences, Sophia's response as an adaptable human will change and she won't experience blind panic whenever her daughter rings and sounds upset.

Apart from the straightforward 'shock' of being woken at night by telephone, many of us find such calls very distressing because at other times when there've been nightime phone calls they almost certainly weren't good news. The human mind is trying to serve us well: it groups experiences together and searches for ways to handle them, often at a subconscious level - using what has been learned from previous experiences. Sometimes this causes us to react in ways that might be inappropriate - unless we can gradually gain an insight into *why* we're reacting to certain situations in particular ways.

So not only are we buffeted by our responses to external stimuli, sometimes we have a hard time as our own subconscious, in an effort to protect us, actually leads us into reactions that may not 'fit' the present situation - even if they were experienced in situations in the past. So learning to effectively deal with our emotions means not only

> vii   finding strategies to deal with the responses to current stimuli or events, including both the mixed emotions we may feel and the 'background' emotions from longer lasting or significant challenges
>
> *but it also means*
>
> viii   being able to reflect on why we react as we do, and learning over time to filter out the inappropriate reactions which actually stem from past experience.

It's no wonder it can seem so tough to manage emotions effectively, even as adults!

Resilience

There are times when we're experiencing lots of positive emotions, when we may feel that nothing negative can touch us. Clearly it's not true: we would all be affected by a sudden tragedy. But feeling happy and positive about life in general can definitely offer a degree of protection from some of the everyday negative or frustrating events. I know when I've felt happy and settled both at work and in my family life it's a lot easier to be positive and cope with the minor irritations and frustrations which are just part of life, especially when I'm healthy, well-rested, and with no underlying worries about anything in particular. Personality, support and background may also play a part, but positive emotions not only make us feel good - like the stereotype of someone in love going around smiling all the time - but from a simple biochemical basis upwards, they help us be more resilient to some of the negative emotional stimuli we come across.

The opposite is also true. If we are experiencing a lot of negative emotions, perhaps from being stressed or frustrated with what's happening in our lives, then our resilience to other events is likely to be less. If we have established ways of taking care of our own emotional health by ensuring we can express emotions appropriately, and find and make good use of support, then we'll be able to build resilience. There'll be more on building resilience later (p.102).

Suppression and expression

In terms of personality, there are huge differences in how we handle emotions. Some folk seem to always appear the same, no matter what's going on, whereas others seem rocked by every event. We'd probably all be able to locate ourselves on that spectrum - our family, friends and colleagues might have a view too! But to make sure that we can do our job effectively, we have all had to learn how to handle the emotions we experience every day in the best possible way. Expressing our positive emotions or feelings - telling someone we care about them, are delighted in their success, giving our own good news with a big smile - is often easier than expressing negative emotions like anger or frustration in a manner which is appropriate.

Often we have one of two responses to unhappy or difficult emotions which we either bury or feel overwhelmed by. Culturally, in a historical sense, British people have had the stiff upper lip approach, and for many of us there may still be a tendency to bury anything that might disrupt our equilibrium; our working environments can reinforce this. In fact some adults will have been told when they were growing up that the right thing to do is to be strong and not 'show' emotion, perhaps particularly boys. That's obviously not true for everyone and there are others (or the same people at different times) who seem to want or need to express every emotion they have - leaving others in no doubt about what they're feeling. We probably all know someone who is very emotionally expressive; we know within a minute of them walking in the room what their mood is, for good or ill, in terms of the atmosphere they generate around them. We all have to acknowledge that our emotional state will impact the people round us, and that we have a responsibility for the atmosphere of feelings we create. Perhaps we can all identify with the person who when asked, says they are fine, but everyone around knows that isn't the case because their reactions clearly tell a different story: we probably also all have experience of the drama queen! But we all need to be very clear that every individual (yes, including ourselves!) brings something to the emotional atmosphere of a situation.

REFLECTIVE ACTIVITY

⇨   Think for a moment about what close friends or colleagues would say
      about the way you contribute to the emotional atmosphere of a place.
      Is it the same at home and in your place of work, or different?

⇨   If you feel brave enough, you can even ask people!

It's worth pointing out that suppressing emotions isn't the same as 'holding' them. Imagine if you are upset that you weren't given the promotion you'd hoped for: you may feel upset, tearful, frustrated or angry. However, you may decide not to express your feelings at work but wait until you are alone or at home or with trusted friends to express the emotions you feel about the event. Suppressing emotions, on the other hand, is a bit like keeping a lid on a steaming kettle. When we supress a feeling we keep on *not* expressing it, we think we should forget it, *'it's not worth it'*, or think we can (or should) just press on regardless. So in the example above, waiting until an appropriate time and expressing the disappointment, anger, regret, or frustration that not getting the job caused is fine, as long as those feelings are expressed at some point and not just bottled up. Suppressing emotions, especially negative ones like anger, or rejection can lead to later problems, both psychological and physical. Essentially emotions *do* need to be expressed but in a way and at a time that's appropriate for the individual and the situation they are in. Crying at a funeral, or at a sad film or in a hospital or in lots of other situations is perfectly acceptable. Breaking down repeatedly at work or out shopping, less so. There is a difference between supressing an emotion which means it *isn't* expressed or often not even recognised, and learning to manage our emotions so that we *can* express them at times and in places and in ways that feel safe and appropriate, allowing us to access the support and reflection time we need.

Managing emotions

Managing emotions is about being able to express what we are feeling in an appropriate way that allows us to release the emotion safely, without causing further distress for either ourselves or others, and finding a way to begin to process and think about what the emotion is all about and what might need, if anything, to be done. There is a recognisable process for doing this that we may realise we follow more or less, though may not have identified as such. As you read through, try to hold in mind real scenarios of what *you've* done and how *you've* coped with recent emotional situations. To get you started, try thinking about the scenario below.

REFLECTIVE ACTIVITY

⇨   Many people have some kind of phobia: often it might be irrational,
    but none the less induces a strong reaction, not just a distaste or fear
    that is shared by everyone.

⇨   If you have a phobia or strong aversion to something, spend a moment thinking
    about how you would feel if you were faced with the thing or situation you avoid.
    Think about the physical feelings, and the emotions.
    What you would do if you were in that situation and what you would do
    afterwards when 'danger' had passed.

STAGE 1 ACKNOWLEDGE THE FEELINGS

The first stage in managing anything is to recognise that it is exists, and acknowledge it. Even this can be hard sometimes: we're complex organisms, and often experience multiple emotions at the same time. It's useful to remind ourselves that all emotions affect us, often physically, so a primary indicator of what we're feeling is from our physical 'symptoms,' though our mental and emotional 'state' can also give us clues. Think about worry or stress for example: if we're worried, we may feel 'butterflies', a dry mouth, struggle to concentrate or sleep, not feel much like eating, and may withdraw a bit from social engagements. More extreme worry may cause our heart to race, our pupils to dilate and all the other aspects of our fight-or-flight response may come into play. That's an acute stress response. It may not be comfortable but isn't essentially damaging, unless it's repeated too frequently: whereas chronic stress (less extreme but lasting longer) can have numerous negative health consequences.

If we think about *distress* rather than *stress*, on the other hand, we'll recognise that this involves feeling sad and tearful, full of sorrow, fed up, unable to cope. This can lead to feeling apathetic about doing anything, crying, shutting ourselves away, or in extreme cases where the distress becomes chronic, finding that almost every 'function' of our lives has been affected. And when it comes to anger, we may want to shout, state things as we see them, give people a piece of our mind, and if we're very angry and frustrated we may want to lash out and hurt someone, possibly enjoy planning their demise? We may feel a tight knot in our stomachs, find ourselves unable *not* to think about it, hard to relax, we may even want to pace about. If we're happy however, we usually smile a lot, have a spring in our step, feel that nothing is too much effort and feel a deep sense of satisfaction and often a physical sensation of wellbeing and pleasure in life.

REFLECTIVE ACTIVITY

⇨ Take moment to consider what you are feeling right now.

⇨ Think first about your body - what sensations you have, bearing in mind that usually we will be experiencing several concurrently. You may feel sleepy but also want a drink or decide that you are cold. You may have a gnawing feeling in your stomach because you are worried - or eyes that ache from reading.

⇨ Think also about your mental state.
Did you start reading this book because you were relaxed and curious or because you were concerned about a particular pupil or perhaps, actually, to put off a chore? Perhaps you are experiencing several 'background' emotions, worry about work or a friend, anger at someone.
Work out how you recognise and acknowledge your various feelings.

Sometimes we may have good insight into what's going on. I might know I'm feeling fragile because I am really worried about ageing parents who are becoming increasingly frail, or some personal physical symptom I am finding it more and more difficult to ignore. I may be able to recognise that I am still angry about an argument I had with my partner earlier in the day, which I know is not 'resolved'.

At other times we don't really know why we seem to be in a particular kind of emotional space, and it may take time to realise the cause. Either way, once we've acknowledged the emotion, simply recognising that we 'feel' a particular way, we still have to move onto the next stage - that of expressing and coping with the feelings.

STAGE 2 FEEL THE FEELINGS FULLY

Many people have developed ways of not letting themselves feel the emotion. Often we'll brush it off, but actually the feelings are important - *we can actually only express an emotion we have allowed ourselves to feel*. Some perspective may be helpful, not making a drama out of something relatively minor for example, *but still* it remains important to allow ourselves to feel what's happening. If something happens that makes us feel sad we need to express it, but we can only do that when we are in touch with it - when we feel it. It's not at all uncommon when something very tragic happens to not be able to express the sadness straightaway. Following a trauma like a death or an accident there are often a lot of things to do, and in such times it can be hard to let ourselves 'feel' the feelings until some of the busyness has calmed down. If the busyness continues, it can be a bit tough to get back in touch with the feeling, though often talking about it will mean the emotions come to the surface once again. One very common response to significant events is indeed to talk about them, which is usually beneficial. Circumstances often dictate that we 'hold' emotions for a time, but they will never be effectively dealt with or managed until we have acknowledged their existence and given ourselves the chance to feel them.

What stops us sometimes is a misplaced belief that 'feeling' them somehow weakens us - back to that stiff upper lip belief. But what we now know is that dealing effectively with our emotions actually aids our emotional and physical wellbeing. Every feeling is valid: if we feel it, it's true for us, at that time, even when we tell ourselves, or others may tell us, that we are taking things too seriously, or being somehow unbalanced about it. Some feelings may be misplaced - we might feel guilty about something that wasn't our fault for example, but the feeling is valid if we feel it - it may not be justified, it may be misplaced but it is still valid if it is there. Remember our emotions are responses to stimuli; they are not usually under our conscious control. But we may be able to exercise some control over how we respond to them. Responding to what we feel demands that we first acknowledge and *feel* the emotion.

STAGE 3 EXPRESS THE FEELINGS

If we were lucky, we would have had parents who had the emotional know-how, the language skills and the resources to help us learn to express feelings, giving us comfort when necessary and encouragement to tell them what we were feeling and what was happening. They would have helped us to think about our feelings and perhaps even suggested ways we might respond, so that we learned to soothe ourselves to a degree but also to seek comfort and support when we needed it.

But this is a gradual process and it is not finished in childhood: it's something we continue to do for most of our lives. Learning to express our emotions appropriately is less like riding a bike (once learned, never forgotten) and more like practising yoga. If we keep on practising we can improve, little by little, learning when we need to seek support, taking some time to ourselves or having a good cry, learning how to articulate what's happening and going on to the next stage, that of reflecting on the experience (*see below*).

Of course expressing emotions - crying when upset, telling someone you feel angry at what they have done, letting someone know you're feeling afraid or highly anxious for example, may not always be comfortable. Often we wish that whatever happened to cause the feelings simply hadn't happened: but it did, and we responded, and the only way to get 'beyond' this is to acknowledge it, feel it fully and express it. As adults we usually (but by no means always) express our emotions appropriately. The expression of emotion (with their accompanying physical sensations) can leave us exhausted and lead to other emotions, we may start off by expressing our anger over something but then find ourselves crying, with frustration or disappointment. And many of us will only be able to express emotions when we feel safe enough to do so - we tend to 'hold' emotions until we feel safe, for example perhaps rushing home after something has upset us, literally biting back tears until we are in a place where we can let the emotion we are feeling out.

> ## REFLECTIVE ACTIVITY
> ⇨   Think for a moment about what 'safe' means for you, in terms of expressing emotions.
> ⇨   Is it being alone or with others?
> ⇨   Does the place matter?
> ⇨   Are there particular people you seek out if you knew you needed to let go of certain feelings?

Obviously people vary in the ways they express emotion and in the places and people that make them feel safe enough to do so. But the important point is that expression needs to happen in some way so we can move forward. If it doesn't happen at or the near the time we feel it, there's a possibility the feelings just disappear: but generally they build up and will almost certainly spill over at another time. If we can be honest we have probably all experienced times when we have been unfair to someone at work, either a student or another staff member, because we haven't processed our own emotions effectively. Or perhaps we have tried to put a brave face on things and come into work only to find ourselves struggling not to burst into tears or snap at everyone.

Learning to manage our emotions effectively will not only keep us healthy as individuals but will also mean that we don't contribute in unhelpful ways to situations because of our own 'emotional temperature' and cause problems for others around us. Also, as we'll discuss later in this chapter, we will be much better placed to help others who may be struggling with emotions themselves.

STAGE 4 DEAL WITH THE PHYSICAL IMPACT

As I mentioned earlier, many emotions create physical effects as well as feelings, and sometimes these too need to be given some kind of outlet. Many of us will have experienced the inability to sit still after an emotional situation, or even the need to sleep - opposite ends of the spectrum, but they can both be part of the physical impact of experiencing and expressing emotions. Of course they aren't the only possible effects. We may have a desire to talk, or a need for solitude or silence: we may be left with 'energy' we want to get rid of, and need to do something physical like run or walk: we may want to curl up and find something nurturing or simply get fresh air and a change of scene. It varies from one individual to another and will also be different for each of us at different times. What we need to recognise for ourselves and for the students we work with is that often physical feelings don't just vanish when emotions or feelings have been expressed. We need to think about how this can happen safely and appropriately. In general, in school, we may need to provide some space before pupils who have expressed their feelings are ready to resume what they were doing, with a recognition that this is natural.

STAGE 5 REFLECTION

Almost any aspect of growth and learning involves reflection, and it's no different when we think about managing emotions. When the emotional storm has passed, once we've completed the stages of acknowledging, fully feeling and expressing the emotions and physical effects, then we often come to a time when we can think more clearly about what has happened. Sometimes we think - was it really as bad as it seemed? Maybe it was; but after we've safely acknowledged and expressed emotions caused by the situation, we may see it a little differently. When we feel calmer, we may be able to be more rational. It's also useful to think about how our own responses might have added to the situation.

Pete was a newly qualified teacher and new to the role of form tutor: he was also in the middle of moving house and his father had just been diagnosed with cancer. He was generally liked and respected by most of the young people in his teaching and tutor groups at the secondary school but one pupil, Danesh, he found particularly difficult to deal with.

Danesh was living with his mother, but had previously spent time in care due to his mother's mental illness. Danesh generally exuded a distrust for anyone in authority and often came across as aggressive. It was the second week for Pete as form tutor, and despite numerous chats with Danesh he was continuing to arrive late. Usually Pete would just get him to sit down and chat to him at the end of the session but on this particular day, Pete was feeling pretty fed up generally and frustrated by Danesh and his lateness, and challenged him as soon as he walked into the classroom. When Pete asked him why he was late, Danesh simply shrugged. Pete said there would be consequences for lateness and Danesh shrugged again.

Pete was aware this was all playing out in from of his new form group. In an effort to show his authority, Pete raised his voice telling him not to be so rude and to give an explanation. Danesh turned to leave the classroom, his usual strategy when faced with a confrontation and Pete shouted more loudly, telling him not to walk away when he was speaking. Danesh turned, picked up the nearest item he could find (sadly an empty chair) and launched it to the front of the class where it narrowly missed Pete. As a result, Danesh was excluded from school. What Pete didn't know until later, because Danesh had resolutely refused to tell him, was that he was late because he was dropping off his younger sister at school before he went to school because his mother couldn't get up.

It is worth pointing out here that this is not meant to be a criticism of Pete. He is a good teacher but he is a human being doing the best job he could on any given day. As humans we can all look back to situations where we could have done things differently.

REFLECTIVE ACTIVITY

⇨   Think for a moment about how this could have played out differently.

⇨   What factors may have influenced Pete to react as he did on this particular day?

⇨   What could Pete have done differently?

⇨   What else could have been done differently to avoid what happened?

So an important component of the reflection process is to look at our responses, and think about what other alternatives there might have been. Maybe Pete hadn't had time to process his emotions about his father, and he was probably experiencing the heightened anxiety common to many people in a new role. We will never know if the situation would have been better if Pete hadn't issued the challenge to Danesh and in any case, sometimes a challenge is essential. For it to play out in front of a class often pushes both parties to react in more extreme ways. Perhaps if Pete had been able to chat to a colleague before the lesson, it might have helped, though I know there is too often no time for this. Perhaps if Danesh had had a key adult who could have met with him at the beginning of the day and knew the family situation better (Bombèr 2011), he wouldn't have become so stressed. Many possibilities. As we saw earlier, it's so often the build-up of lots of different 'stressors' that can cause us to act as we do, and our emotional state will equally often influence the way we act or react.

But another important aspect of reflection is that we can really only think about *our own personal contribution* to situations, consider our own reactions and perhaps some of our motives. There may be a time when it's useful, perhaps after specific incidents as a de-brief, to consider how situations could have been differently managed as a group. But reflection is most definitely *not* a process by which we should apportion blame. All too often in de-brief situations, the process becomes one of cross-questioning and blame, which only really serves the purpose of raising everyone's tension and anxiety. Dealing with situations that may be highly charged in an emotional sense will be more of a challenge if the parties involved are feeling anxious or stressed - feeling that they're being watched and judged.

So it may be helpful to involve others in reflection. But sometimes it's most useful to ask ourselves why we acted as we did and try to understand our own motives and 'drivers'. The purpose isn't to beat ourselves up or give ourselves a hard time about the fact that we could have done things differently, but to grow in our self-awareness and find new and better ways to learn to deal with situations and emotions in a more effective way. This will enable us to be healthy, well-rounded adults, as well as practitioners who can behave professionally even when under pressure.

Crucially, we need to understand how we process our emotions and how if that doesn't happen effectively they may 'spill' into other situations. We may not be the only party experiencing emotions but we may, by virtue of the fact that we are functioning adults and professionals, be one of the few who can effectively 'manage' our emotions, and reflect on them. The hope is that over time we can develop a shared language to ensure that we can help others, especially our pupils, to learn to do the same.

STAGE 6 REFRAMING

Life is a learning process, and little by little experiences change us and how we see the world, how we view or 'frame' situations and people, and even how we view and frame ourselves. Reflection will lead us to a position where we can *re-frame* how we see ourselves, our responses, and other people. For example, a person who has experienced others' anger or violence in response to their own feelings may have learned to suppress their emotions. It will only be through experiencing others and then themselves expressing emotions and being responded to in ways that are not violent or angry, that they will be able to re-frame how they see emotional expression and responses to that expression.

Many reading this will probably be aware of the emotion of shame and how it can be an almost ever-present feeling for children and young people who have experienced difficulties with attachment or trauma. In some of our pupils then, emotional expression can lead to a sense of shame. Many of us who are regarded as well-adjusted will have glimpsed this feeling after we have expressed emotions, perhaps been angry, or tearful when we didn't expect to be, perhaps not behaving the way we usually would. At the very least we can feel awkward and may find ourselves apologising. So reflection can usefully involve some direction for reframing and even some practical ways to manage the aftermath of emotions.

Sarah was working as a TA at a local college. One day, unfortunately, she 'snapped' and became very angry during a dispute with another member of staff in the department. The next day she didn't turn up for work or phone in, and after a few days the head of department rang her. Sarah had assumed she'd been fired for her outburst. The head of department explained that she hadn't been fired and she still had a job, though they would need to help her develop some strategies to deal with situations more appropriately in the future. It transpired later that Sarah had in fact grown up in care and had been through a number of foster care placements before being placed in a residential home. She had also been fired from several jobs for angry outbursts before she engaged with therapy and had since studied and travelled. But she still assumed that the response she would get following a heated quarrel was the end of a relationship as that had so often been her experience in the past. The notion of restoring the relationship and working on alternative ways of behaving wasn't how she framed the situation.

Reframing or changing perspective doesn't happen with just one instance, but whenever there is reflection there is an open door for some reframing to take place.

So to manage our emotions, we need to

ix   acknowledge our feelings,

x   allow ourselves to feel them fully

xi   express them appropriately when it feels safe for us to do so, including physical effects

xii   consider the contribution that our own 'emotional' state may have on our responses to situations we find ourselves in, re-frame and look at alternative strategies.

The impact of stress

Having looked at the 'process' of managing emotions it will be helpful now to look at one particular feeling we all experience to a greater or lesser extent - stress. It is also something which nearly all vulnerable or troubled children or young people will experience, so we need to think about how we manage it and how the way we do this impacts how we deal with other emotions.

Stress is an experience we all feel, seemingly increasingly. It not only causes temporary feelings and physical changes, but can also create damaging longer-term physical changes and emotional habits. Stress is a growing problem within our society and especially for people working in school environments. Difficulty in managing our emotions can cause additional stress which will have a negative impact, not only on us as individuals but on the people who live and work with us, with the potential to damage relationships or cause further emotional difficulties for others.

REFLECTIVE ACTIVITY

⇨ Try to remember a recent occasion when you felt stressed in the school context.

⇨ List some of the feelings you experienced.

⇨ List some of the ways stress may have caused you to react differently
   from the way you would normally react.
   Were you less tolerant of others? Did your mind wander when you were
   listening to someone, or did you become very talkative?
   Become agitated or very still?
   Try to be specific about yourself and the way you react.

⇨ How did you deal with this?

⇨ What great stress management strategies do you have?

I imagine that words like distracted, irritable, snappy, and possibly antagonistic or aggressive may have come to mind, or perhaps panic, sadness, inability to sit still, alertness, clumsiness, forgetfulness, fidgeting and maybe tearfulness depending on the level of stress. Many of the children and young people in our schools who are 'troubled' will be experiencing fairly extreme emotions and may lack the strategies to deal with them. They may suppress and internalise many of their feelings which can be very damaging for later mental health, or they may be expressed inappropriately, for example a child who is angry, hurts another child or throws things. Such pupils and students may also be suffering from pretty high levels of stress.

So if as adults we can understand what *we* do that enables us to express and process stress and emotions safely, we can then explain this to our pupils explicitly, and model it for them in the moment, perhaps giving them alternative ways to cope with how *they* feel and to combat some of the negative impact stress has on them (*and see* p.170).

> *Jaden* was ten and his parents had recently separated. He missed his father, who he hardly ever saw, even though his older brother had gone to live with their father. Since the separation Jaden had become quite volatile and one day arrived looking sullen: within minutes he had punched another child who made a comment about his trainers.
>
> A he walked with a member of staff (a young male NQT) to the 'inclusion' room, the adult was heard to say that sometimes when he felt really angry, he kicked a football against a wall - a simple, empathic and sensitive way of offering an alternative strategy.

Sometimes simply offering or flagging up an idea from an appropriate example in your own life can sow a seed they may try later on (*and see* Chapter 8 *for more*).

Managing inappropriate expressions of emotion

Of course we need to deal with inappropriate expressions of emotion from our pupils, in such a way that we give clear messages. The messages we give must recognise that the emotions or feelings are entirely valid; if someone feels something, then that is real for them. No feeling can be wrong, and expressing such emotions is acceptable, in fact essential, as we saw earlier in the chapter. However everyone must learn to express feelings in a way that doesn't hurt others. The practicality of venting anger through kicking a ball against a wall at that moment is almost irrelevant. The important point is that the adult *validated the feeling and the need for its expression*, and gave a suggestion, empathically: no doubt as they spent time in the inclusion room many more suggestions would be discussed together, once the young person was soothed and relaxed, and able to be more receptive (hearing is reduced when someone is seriously stressed, so they are unlikely to take anything in).

The young person may have remained silent and upset to an extent, but he was being given empathy for his feelings and some strategies. Once he was relaxed, he would be encouraged to come up with his own. There was not a pretence that everything was OK, or that it wasn't OK to 'feel' the emotion. The discussion hopefully centred on *how to deal with those feelings*. This can happen informally as well as in lessons, but when feelings are expressed inappropriately we need to give children empathy (for the feeling, not the actions) and alternatives: otherwise it's like marking work and saying it's wrong without any hints as to why or what the right answer might be.

Many of us do have effective strategies to manage stress and distress. The important point here is that we not only need to continue to do this effectively but we also need to know what we're doing, so that we can model how we manage it for the children and young people we work with.

Modelling appropriate expressions of emotion

As society we seem to give mixed messages about appropriate emotional expression. Some reality TV shows seem to manipulate situations to 'capture' emotional expressions - the X Factor being a prime example: but in lots of other walks of life, expressing how we feel can be difficult because it is not expected. How many times do people ask us how we are? And yet we know they are absolutely one hundred per cent expecting us to say *"Fine"*. If we didn't, they may be unsure how to respond and it would certainly feel awkward. On other occasions, people do really want to know how we are, and whilst I am not suggesting that we bare our souls with everyone, neither should we always live behind a fake smile. *Acknowledging* an emotion is important even if we don't express it at that time. So in answer to the *"How are you?"* question we could easily say,

> Actually I've been having a tough time recently, but I've got some great support so I'm getting by. Thanks for asking though.

> Actually things are really difficult now and I know now isn't the time but I'd value a chat sometime.

… or any one of a number of other responses in addition to the *"Fine"* which of course is also appropriate sometimes.

If we are to create cultures of care within schools, it starts with us, with the adults, the leaders, being concerned with each other as staff and colleagues, noticing and acknowledging and getting used to dialogues about emotions. Only through doing this can we create environments where we can support children and young people with their own emotions.

But what is even more difficult than talking about emotions generally is talking about emotions specifically: our emotions, our feelings and what *we* do to express them safely and appropriately, and how we withstand the exhaustion that may accompany them. Somehow that seems a lot harder: we have to be really comfortable and secure in our own ability to manage our emotions and have good self-esteem in order to speak freely about our experiences, and what does and doesn't work for us.

Even those of us who are very in tune with our emotions and have learned to manage them effectively will, because we are human, have times when our strategies fail and we don't express them appropriately. Being secure enough to talk about these times is even more of a challenge. But this is precisely what our pupils need, adults who are willing and able to talk openly about emotions, to share with them how we cope with our own feelings and to be able to be honest about the times when we can't, and what we do then.

If we do have effective strategies, it can still be useful to note these down and consider which ones are suitable for sharing in a particular context: so, for example, a long solitary walk, or a brisk run after work, may be very effective for some of us but they may not strategies that can be used easily by our pupils, especially not here and now in school.

REFLECTIVE ACTIVITY

⇨ Jot down about four different emotions you have experienced in the last week or so.

⇨ Then for each one, note down one of the ways you expressed them. Perhaps you wrote a 'strongly worded letter of complaint', if you were cross about a service or product, perhaps you cheered yourself up with a treat, if you felt upset by something, maybe you sought out a trusted friend for a rant, or maybe you delayed going home one day to ensure you didn't take out your feelings inappropriately on your family.

Whilst noting down your strategies, it is also helpful to think about how you *feel about* what you do: some people find they have feelings about the strategies they use to manage their emotions! Which can sometimes be as much of a challenge as the emotions themselves. Sometimes our strategies to relieve one type of stress can even become a different source of stress.

Arlene's mother had dementia and several nights after work she would go to see her in the nursing home. Arlene always felt both upset and guilty after she had seen her. She had talked to a few friends about her feelings and said she really struggled to go home afterwards because her husband was always trying to be supportive but somehow that upset her even more. She started calling round to different 'mates' houses after she'd been to see her mother for a quick drink before going home. Her husband of course found it difficult that she could feel supported by drinking with a mate, but was effectively shutting him out.

One evening, a particularly close friend suggested to Arlene that she simply explained to her husband that what she needed was just to go home and not talk about her mother or her feelings unless she wanted to. So simple. It worked and prevented tensions growing in their relationship whilst giving her the support she needed which was to not talk.

If we are to be able to model ways of effectively managing our emotions for the children and young people we work with we need to be able to recognise the strategies we use ourselves and we need to be able to discuss these in ways which are straightforward, explicit and honest.

Taking your own temperature

Sometimes the way that we recognise that something is actually an 'issue' for us is when we talk about it. If we're to help children and young people by talking about and modelling strategies we might use when dealing with our own emotions we need to be sure that we are actually OK to do this without it causing an emotional reaction for ourselves. Words are incredibly powerful and often stating something aloud is a way of making it very real. That is why sometimes it's tough to tell people about a breakup, a bereavement or a disappointment of some kind. It's very possible to discuss strategies for managing emotions without necessarily discussing what caused them, *but* if a young person asks, then we need to be prepared to be open at least to a degree, or any authenticity can be lost.

Carol was a warm-hearted, skilled and experienced TA in an SEMH school and students would often gravitate towards her if they were feeling upset or anxious. She had a very calming approach and this would often rub off on the students as soon as they entered her room which was regarded as an emotional oasis by many.

It was surprise one day to find her in tears in the office. Over a cuppa she explained that she had tried to help a young female student who had issues with her self-esteem and would often have panic attacks. She had spent some time with the student over the course of several days explaining some particular breathing exercises which she said had helped her own daughter when she'd been going through a difficult time. On this particular day the student had asked why her daughter had been having a difficult time and Carol explained that she had been violently assaulted one night on the way home. Somehow saying it out loud unleashed a wave of emotion for Carol. It had happened some years previously, but clearly there was still pain attached to it for her, understandably, and suddenly there she was struggling to manage her own emotions whilst trying to help the student. In retrospect, she might have been better to describe the incident in less evocative terms, something Carol might think about for another time; in the present though, she simply needed support from a colleague.

Being professional doesn't mean that we are robots. We will all experience emotions and generally it's not wrong to be honest about these. However our purpose in working with those pupils who are struggling to manage their emotions, or who are feeling stressed, angry, anxious or upset, is to be warm, nurturing and kind, as well as boundaried and professional. Witnessing others being upset can be upsetting and the pupils we deal with are likely to have encountered all sorts of unhelpful ways adults use to deal with emotions. We want to show them effective strategies that are also appropriate, ones they can adopt and use if they find them helpful. If in the process of doing that we become very emotional ourselves, it's likely to confuse things for them.

We are human. If things don't work out as planned then we need to be kind to ourselves, not beat ourselves up. But we also need to learn for the future and testing our emotional temperature by talking about things with other adults *before* sharing stratgies with our students can be very helpful.

As individuals we all have many different ways to manage emotions but to explore just a few of the myriad ideas and possibilities out there, take a look at the chart.

THINGS WHICH CAN HELP AT A STRESSFUL TIME	GENERAL RESILIENCE BUILDING ACTIVITIES
Stepping away from the situation (if possible) *Having a moment of quiet* *A few deep breaths* *A specific calming activity* *Going for a quick walk outside* *Chatting to a colleague* *Sharing humour* *Having a drink or snack in a quiet place* *Agreeing a shared 'emotional' language to describe and label feelings (described later)*	*Building in the basics to look after yourself* *Good food, enough sleep, some regular exercise* *Some regular time to relax doing something you like to do* *Leaning specific techniques or habits that help you - yoga, mindfulness, meditation, tapping (see also Chapter 6)* *Having some time when you can talk openly with someone you trust and who understands* *Having close relationships that support you as a person*

Developing a shared language

I'd like to look now at how we can develop and use a shared language to begin a dialogue about feelings and emotions and then at how strategies for healthy and explicit expression can be modelled for the children and young people we work with each day. When people have shared experiences and a shared language, communication is much easier.

I was talking with a Head teacher I've known for many years about the stress of inspection. We were speaking at the conclusion of a successful inspection of her school. I asked about her partner's response the week previously to the news of the impending OFSTED visit. She explained he hadn't known when the visit was happening, but when she walked through the door that night, he said simply - *"I guess you've had the call then?"*

Our lives evolve and develop through communicating with all sorts of people, many of whom don't have the same shared experience that we do, or even the same language. Communicating in those circumstances is a bit tougher. It's great when we don't need to be explicit, when we can make a vague suggestion or a veiled comment and people get what we mean and respond in the way we might hope for. Or even better when a look, or a gesture means we are understood. In the example above, just this woman's demeanour as she walked through the door communicated her mood, and from that her partner was able to deduce what had happened, because he knew about 'her world'. It would be fair to assume that he knew that an inspection was on the cards and that this was something she would find stressful. So this knowledge combined with her demeanour meant it wasn't that difficult to work out what had happened. No words necessary.

Great, when it's possible, usually only in very close relationships: it certainly isn't the way that communication usually happens. Interpretation is almost always involved in communication, and the way we interpret things often depends on how we are feeling ourselves. In addition, when we communicate, the words are only a small proportion of our message. The rest will be communicated with our tone and gestures and these will be affected by our own emotions, how we are feeling at the time.

We have all had experiences when someone has said something but there has been a mismatch between what they have said and the message that was communicated. In a staff room we can usually tell if a colleague's lesson hasn't gone well by the way they enter the room: we may choose to enquire, to offer support or not, and that's down to our own state of mind and possibly our relationship with that colleague. But the 'message' on such occasions is unmistakable.

Until we can learn to be honest about our own emotions with other adults, it may be a tall order to talk openly with the children and young adults we work with day to day in school. The first step is to manage our emotions. The next is to develop a shared lexicon for talking about feelings, one which allows us to communicate about emotions with each other easily and effectively, so that we can then conduct effective conversations with children and young people about how *they* can express their feelings and emotions in ways that allow supportive dialogue with adults who may be able to offer strategies that could help them further.

There are a few emotions that are acknowledged across cultures: love, hate, sorrow, joy and fear. But we also must remember that in Ancient Greece there were at least five different words to describe different types of love, for example, whereas in our language we have just one.

*When **Shanika** was taken into care at aged eight she had to move areas and start a new school. Staff noticed that she was quiet and withdrawn a lot of the time and would resist all attempts by other children to engage her. At playtimes she would find a quiet corner and stand there watching the other children play.*

Various staff members asked if she was OK, did she want to talk, or tried to jolly her along and get her to join in. One day a student teacher simply went to stand near her. After a few minutes the student teacher said that sometimes when she felt sad she didn't want to be with others.

Shanika said immediately that she wasn't sad, she just missed her friends and didn't want new friends. She wanted her old friends back.

Is missing friends the same as feeling sad? What Shanika was feeling was that she was missing her friends. Of course she was probably also missing her parents, her home, her siblings and a thousand other close familiar things that she lost when she came into care. In that situation many of us would describe ourselves as feeling sad. People might use slightly different words and in many ways the words don't matter as much as the fact that they express what is happening for us.

Words are certainly not the only way we communicate; gestures, tone, looks can all communicate a message but words are undoubtedly important. Often it is through words that we express feelings and those expression can bring about a relief - a problem shared so often is a problem halved. Acknowledging that something is a problem may indeed be the first step to dealing with it and is an important element in lots of counselling methodologies. I'm not suggesting for one minute that schools or classrooms become places where we spend all day asking how each other 'how we are' and labelling every feeling or emotion we have as we go through the day. But I am saying that when dealing with troubled children and young people it is helpful to both the staff and the pupils if the adults are able to talk openly about feelings and emotions, because that is a key way of communicating about important information and strategies with the troubled member of the class.

The first step is simply to develop 'words' to describe feelings - the amount will depend on the age of the pupils or students you work with and remember that older students who are on the spectrum of trouble will not always have the knowledge or ability to recognise and label their feelings that others their age might.

REFLECTIVE ACTIVITY

It can be helpful to do this activity with someone else

⇨ Note down names of common emotions and feelings and without using a dictionary try define them.

⇨ Think about the physical expressions of each that you have mentioned.

⇨ Then think about what you do if you saw someone who seemed to be expressing that emotion and discuss how you might react.

⇨ The following case studies give some ideas of how language can be used to describe what you think a child might be feeling

What might you do if you felt this way?

Consider things they might find helpful.

Delai was a Year 2 child who had experienced numerous traumatic events in a very short period of time. Over a few weeks in his new school a pattern emerged of quite violent outbursts directed towards whoever happened to be in the way. He was usually quite an articulate child. When Delai had his third half-day exclusion a meeting was called to discuss alternative ways of managing the situation.

When he was re-admitted it was explained to him that he would be taken out of the last part of each lesson to work with a member of staff on a special project, which worked out at about ten minutes every hour/hour and a half. While his outbursts didn't always happen at the end of the lesson, it was the time when they often occurred.

The special project started simply with a session about what happens in our body

when we feel angry. The staff member started by explaining that she sometimes got angry, she gave some examples, and even confessed that she sometimes felt angry when children hurt each other. She talked about racing hearts, wanting to throw things and shared with him what she did; remove herself from the situation, went to a safe place and use one of her 'tricks,' breathing in to a count of seven and out to a count of 11, or colouring. They developed a series of signals they could watch for that showed either of them were starting to feel angry.

There wasn't an overnight miracle, but Delai never again had three half-day exclusions in one week and during the following half term had none.

__Marget__ was 14 and found herself repeatedly thrown out of lessons for not following instructions and being insolent and rude to teachers. In an attempt to prevent the situation from escalating she was assigned a regular session with the learning mentor. They spent the first few sessions getting to know each other, developing their relationship and discussing impulses and how we usually don't respond to all of our impulses but develop ways of choosing how we behave. Marget herself identified that she couldn't handle direct confrontation without arguing, so even a simple "Marget, take off your coat" seemed to catapult her into a conflict because she would argue.

Marget started by saying she couldn't help herself, but over time with the mentor she developed a script she could use to enable her to give herself a bit of space. It basically involved her saying the word 'yes' within the classroom setting, then noting down what she actually felt - "It was a stupid request, I had only just got into the classroom and I would have sat down in a moment anyway."

Saying yes was extremely hard for her and became a bit of a joke with Marget and the mentor, who was also working really hard with the teachers to explain what was happening and that when Marget repeated the instruction (another strategy she used) she wasn't being cheeky; she was buying herself time so that she didn't launch back into her preferred strategy of arguing.

Jarod (six) was very excitable. He would run everywhere, talk constantly, even when seated he would be constantly moving. He was in many ways like a toddler inside a six-year-old's body. He was always hyper-vigilant and reacted to every stimuli. Jarod had witnessed extreme domestic violence. Numerous strategies were tried but didn't seem to help. One day when he was out of the classroom in an 'inclusion' room the teaching assistant got him to feel his heartbeat. She invited him to do star jumps which made it go even faster, and then sit almost still to see and feel how it came back down.

The TA introduced Jared to the concept of stress and worry and feeling safe. Eventually she was able to teach him how to slow himself down by counting his breaths. His excitability was due in part to his constant worry about what might happen next.

Every day began with a brief time with the TA and she would remind Jared that he was safe in the school and that he could find her if needed to feel extra safe. They developed a way of talking about feeling safe or worried and ways to respond to these feelings.

In all these everyday situations, language was essential. Being able to talk openly about emotions was essential and having strategies to try doing things differently was essential. Anything that has helped you cope with feelings might help a pupil. Anything you have read about, that is appropriate for use with a pupil in a school context, might help a pupil. There is space to be creative, to try things out, providing we work within a culture of empathy and support.

Like the process of learning and acquiring many skills and knowledge, the 'little and often approach' can be helpful. In the classroom, this might mean us simply getting used to referencing our own emotions and encouraging others to do the same, having a class discussion about what happens in our bodies when we feel a particular way, or talking about what we do that helps us deal with a particular emotion or feeling. None of this has to be too contrived, but like anything, when we are trying to do something new it may take a bit of getting used to before it feels 'natural'. For many of us it will feel a bit strange. The culture we live in has definitely changed over recent decades and there is perhaps a greater acceptance of expression of emotion, though there will always be some individuals who find this harder than others. Despite the general move forward we have probably all had a lot of training in not showing our emotions, not talking about them and if at all possible getting so used to squashing them down that we don't even feel them much of the time.

Modelling strategies

The first step is to start labelling emotions, and becoming used to talking about your own feelings with colleagues. The next step is to begin to talk about your emotions with students while also making reference to theirs. This can then be followed by modelling the strategies you use to manage your own.

Adult to pupil

> I am afraid I'm feeling very worried this morning ... my brother is having a serious operation. When I'm worried I know that sometimes I can get a bit short-tempered and snappy. I will try not to, but if I do please be patient and I'll try and make sure that I take a break if think I am going to snap at people.

> You look like you might be feeling a bit sad today. I know what has happened (or not, as the case may be) and I think anyone in your position would feel sad. When I feel sad I sometimes like to sit in a place I like and be on my own: other times I like to talk to someone and tell them about it. What might work best for you?

Some people have said they find it helpful to get used to talking about experiences in the past first, but gradually as it becomes more natural it can be really useful to comment on situations as they arise.

Adult to pupil(s)

> I can remember a time when I would get really angry about … But then someone showed me how I could take a short walk and a few deep breaths and I found that it helped. Shall I show you what I did?

> I am feeling very angry right now about what has just happened and I expect some of you are too. When I feel angry like this (describe the feelings) sometimes it helps me to close my eyes and take a few deep breaths. Perhaps we could all try that right now

Hopefully all the adults can get to the stage where they can comment on the present shared situation and the emotions and feelings that may be apparent, but starting with past events is a good way to begin. With a class, small group or individual, simply asking whether they can remember a time when they felt sad, angry, excited, fearful or worried and then talking about how this feels can be a start. It's a small step after that to talking about how people may be feeling in the present.

Adult to pupil(s)

> I used to get upset when I read sad stories and would sometimes feel myself about to cry. But if I was in a place where I didn't want to, I found that taking a few deep breaths slowly in through my nose would help.

> I am feeling a bit sad today because my dog is ill, it feels hard to concentrate on things, but at break I am going to take a few moments to read my book because I find that helps me when I am worried.

Children and young people who are troubled will probably express emotions in a way that is inappropriate and may hurt others, or at least cause a disturbance in the class. They won't be doing this wilfully; they will be responding to the impact of stimuli and the feeling as well as and on top of the ongoing emotions they are experiencing and had stirred up. As I mentioned above, this response may often be disproportionate to what is actually happening here and now.

Boundaries are important: children and young people need to know what is and is not acceptable. But to punish a child for expressing the inner turmoil they experience seems truly harsh. Surely they need a safe and secure relationship and framework through which they can both receive empathy and then learn to identify what they feel and how to express these feelings and emotions in ways which are safe and appropriate? Empathy and relationships are both crucial. A child or young person will only be able to go from feeling to expression if he or she has received empathy and acceptance first, in relationship, and learnt how to do all these things within that safety which he can later internalise. A lot of children learn some of these skills as toddlers and pre-schoolers in the context of safe loving relationships with parents. But that often won't have been the case for those who are troubled. But they still need to learn those skills and we adults need to teach them what will help.

Quite simply this will be a tall order for a troubled pupil. As adults we need to be clearly accepting of and empathic towards the full range of feelings the child or young person may be experiencing. Without that safety, it would be hard to imagine how the child would feel able to 'express' their feelings. They may still need consequences, but ask yourself whether the student was really 'making a (poor) choice' or whether they were they simply reacting in an impulsive way to overwhelming emotions like fear or panic, and didn't trust that there'd be anyone there to keep them safe whilst they felt like that. The only way they will be able to behave differently is by having the adults they trust showing acceptance and empathy, using explicit language and modelling alternative strategies over time.

HELPING PUPILS LEARN TO MANAGE EMOTION

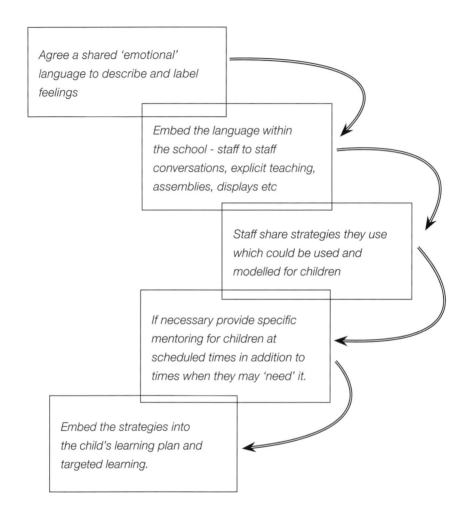

Agree a shared 'emotional' language to describe and label feelings

Embed the language within the school - staff to staff conversations, explicit teaching, assemblies, displays etc

Staff share strategies they use which could be used and modelled for children

If necessary provide specific mentoring for children at scheduled times in addition to times when they may 'need' it.

Embed the strategies into the child's learning plan and targeted learning.

Not making matters worse

Our role as education professionals, whatever the particular individual job title, encompasses a little 'performing'. Whatever else is happening, we will seek to be 'professional', and the 'show must go on'. But it would be naïve to believe or suggest that teachers are never themselves troubled, or show their feelings, sometimes unhelpfully.

We all need to have effective mechanisms to manage our own emotions and anxieties if we're to be able to support the children in our classes who are experiencing 'troubles' and are not ready to learn.

It is also important that we deal appropriately with our feelings to avoid worsening the 'collisions' that may be inevitable when we work with children and young people. Understandably, children who are experiencing powerful emotions are 'charged' a lot of the time. There may be times when they can function well, but a calm exterior can hide the turbulence they are experiencing. If we as the adults don't have strategies to express our own emotions appropriately and deal with our feelings, the risk of an explosive collision increases. I have used the word collision as essentially the child or young person is moving or travelling through their day when they run across something, and a crash or collision of sorts occurs. This concept will be explored more fully in the next chapter.

IN SUMMARY

In this chapter I've looked at what it means to deal effectively with the emotions we all feel and why it's important to do so, not just for our own health and wellbeing but to ensure we can teach the children and young people how to do this through our language and through modelling.

MAIN POINTS

✓   As adults we need to be able to manage our emotions for our own health and wellbeing

✓   This involves acknowledging, feeling, expressing, reflecting on and sometimes reframing our feelings in an appropriate way which doesn't hurt others

✓   We need to learn how to identify and talk about the strategies we use to do this, to support us in working with children and young people

✓   This means that we need a shared language and understanding about emotions and feelings and need to be comfortable in articulating this. If it doesn't exist then explicit teaching can start at any point, with an individual or group

✓   Many of the troubled children and young people will need help in learning how to deal with their feelings and express them appropriately. Staff can model strategies for pupils.

✓   As adults we have a responsibility to manage our emotions effectively so that we don't worsen already volatile situations.

✓   In the next chapter we'll look at the conflicts and collisions that arise in classrooms, consider why these happen and look at ways that we can ensure we don't act in ways that make such situations worse.

CHAPTER 5

Collisions in the classroom

So far we have considered:

how we can create a culture of care

why some of the pupils in our classrooms are not ready to learn

the spectrum of trouble they may be experiencing

AND

how caring for staff enables them to better care for pupils and students

how important it is that we manage our own emotions effectively

SO THAT

we can teach pupils how to manage *their* own emotions

AND TO

make sure we don't make matters worse for pupils who are already struggling with difficult experiences and strong feelings which they express through challenging behaviour.

In this chapter we'll take a closer look at how what I think of as *collisions* can happen in our classrooms, often out the blue, with the potential to cause major disruption to the learning journey of all our pupils.

What happens when a pupil isn't ready to learn?

Staff in schools spend a long time making sure that the classroom environment is conducive to learning, that lessons are planned to make sure pupils learn at the right pace and that pupils who need support have access to what will help them. But all our work can be in vain if the pupils themselves are not ready to learn.

As staff in the classroom, we usually know our pupils. We know the child who always finds numeracy hard, the child who works best at a work station alone rather than on a table with peers, the children who will find work hard if they are together, as they love talking to each other. We will also probably spot the pupil who simply doesn't seem OK on any particular day. But we are human: we can't see everything; and in any case, children in distress may often try to hide their feelings. So, however watchful we are, there will be some pupils who, like a volcano, could be about to erupt at any moment. It can happen at any time: in the playground, in the lunch hall or in a lesson. Something happens and suddenly there is an eruption - a kind of *collision in the classroom*.

The pupil will 'collide' with something. Possibly the teacher, who asks them to be quiet: possibly the teaching assistant who asks if they need help. It may be another pupil who has said something or nudged them, accidentally or otherwise, or taken the seat they were heading for. It could be mention of a particular topic area, or it might even be the pencil point breaking. Whatever it is, something causes the reaction. Pupils who are in a state of readiness to learn may be able to cope with these things happening. Pupils who are not, for whatever reason, may react in ways that are disproportionate and unpredictable.

Thea was six and in a short-term foster placement. Generally she was behaving better at school since she had been in foster care than when she had been with her mother. However, she did like being taken out of the classroom, and would 'manufacture' situations to make sure she would be removed and get to spend time with her dedicated TA in the library or another classroom. So there was a plan to try and deal with situations within the class.

One day when sitting on the mat following playtime, the classroom assistant noticed that Thea was becoming agitated. They were aware that had been a minor incident at playtime but in line with their target of keeping Thea in the classroom, they had not taken her aside. Her agitation increased, and before an adult could even attempt to investigate, Thea bit the girl next to her, kicked the boy on the other side, then picked up a book from a shelf behind her and launched it at the teacher.

Even though staff had sensed that something was wrong and Thea was becoming agitated they didn't anticipate the strength of Thea's reaction. Staff had felt they needed to make some changes to prevent what they thought was another problem developing but perhaps with all the right intentions they were moving at too fast a pace for Thea. Perhaps the decision to ignore the warning signs was, with hindsight, not wise. In fact Thea was absent from school the next day with a virus, so maybe she hadn't been feeling too well. Whatever the particular factors, a collision had occurred. *Children who remain troubled will let us know they are not yet ready to learn under the conditions which we believe are good enough for them*, by their unexpected and possibly even extreme reactions to relatively minor triggers (in this case another little girl telling her at the end of playtime that she, Thea, couldn't join in the game at lunchtime). Thea was communicating: she was telling the adults around her that she needed support - this was evident as she was becoming agitated. She was probably responding to the earlier feelings from playtime - an experience of rejection (when there had probably been many others) and she flipped. But that in itself is a communication.

> **REFLECTIVE ACTIVITY**
>
> ⇨   Take a moment just to think about what other things Thea might have been communicating through her behaviour.

In one particular school where I worked, pupils were generally brought to school in taxis. Simply watching them get out of the taxi could give me an indication of the kind of day they might be going to have. But realising that certainly didn't mean that we could avoid collisions on every occasion. The impact of collisions can be immense, destructive and time-consuming. Even a relatively minor collision takes time to sort out, which either detracts from learning or may often mean that lunchtime won't happen for at least some of the staff involved. More major incidents require form filling, talking to parents, tidying classrooms, and significant mop-up operations. Taking time to reflect on such incidents can help identify emerging patterns.

> **REFLECTIVE ACTIVITY**
>
> ⇨   If you are currently working in a school, think about some of the recent collisions that have happened in your classroom:
>   Were they predictable?
>   What was the trigger?
>   Was the child involved the child who is 'always' involved?

Hazards

Collisions on the road often happen when there is bad weather. In schools the 'bad weather' leading to a collision may be a change in routine, a new teacher, a change of classroom, a new pupil, support staff being absent: even a positive change, like a special visitor or event. But collisions on the road are also more likely when there are problems within the vehicle. Similarly, some children have simply not developed the emotional skills to manage particular situations effectively. They may be unable to 'brake' emotionally. They are the pupils who will have an issue in class but then also on the playground, at lunch and then on the way home. It is easy to see from their behaviour that something is wrong, but it is a lot harder to put it right. If it continues, then they are likely to live up to the expectations that past experience has created: that they will be the one in trouble, the one not learning, the one stopping others from learning.

It's also important to remember that sometimes as adults we have a part to play in such collisions. Sadly, it's often easier to identify what's happened in retrospect, but if I'm honest with myself I know that if I have gone into school not feeling very well, or if I have been anxious or upset, I am more likely to act in ways that may contribute to such collisions. I don't blame myself for it; I am human, and it's simply life, any more than we should be blaming children for what happens with them. But recognising times when we as adults are vulnerable is important in learning how to avoid such collisions, or avoid compounding the chaos such collisions create.

In the last chapter we highlighted the need to manage our emotions effectively. If as an adult I'm stressed because I'm worrying about a forthcoming observation or inspection, I may well be less tolerant, and snap more easily, and this may inflame an already volatile situation. Dealing effectively with our own emotions can reduce the likelihood of that happening. At petrol stations we take care to make sure there are no sparks, because petrol is so highly inflammable. Troubled children will nearly always have supressed, volatile emotions which can behave a bit like petrol: such feelings are quite literally ready to erupt with just a tiny spark. An adult who also has emotions they haven't dealt with effectively may be similar, and their response can create or compound the situation for our pupils. Not a good combination! So it's our responsibility as professionals not to add to the mix.

A clear view

Collisions can't always be avoided. But sometimes they can. We must guard against being so intent on supporting the children we work with by trying to get them to focus, or delivering the lessons we have planned, or on trying to get the child who is out of lessons, again, back into lessons, that we are in effect just watching a car speed headlong past into an inevitably worsening situation. If we do let that happen, we'll also have to spend time dealing with the aftermath.

The better we can be at understanding the 'drivers' or motivators for particular behaviours and the signs of someone losing control, the more able we will be to avoid such collisions, or at least be in a better position to minimise their impact. When there has been an accident on the road, statements are often taken from everyone who witnessed it - simply because they may all have a slightly different perspective on what happened. Some may have seen the incident close at hand, but others may have noticed earlier that there was something on the road or perhaps that there was adverse weather.

In school, in the aftermath of any sort of collision, it's understandable that everyone just wants to put it behind them and move on. But chatting to others who worked with the child during the day can provide additional information which may be helpful in the future, or may at least give some understanding as to why certain things happened. When working as an inclusion officer for a local authority, one of my roles was to be the LA officer present at exclusion hearings. Sadly it was often only at this point that vital information came to light that put a completely different slant on events.

Jamal was a fun-loving, cheeky 11 year old. He did have a temper but this could usually be diffused. He struggled with literacy and had some one-to-one support each morning.

In the afternoon he was in the last lesson and asked if he could go to the literacy support room to print something out. He was told that he could perhaps go later. Jamal didn't work well in the lesson, and so was not allowed to go to do the printing. When the teacher told him he wasn't allowed to go, his reaction was 'off the scale'. Jamal shouted, swore, tipped over desks and squared up to the teacher.

The support teacher he had worked with in literacy had had to leave early to attend a meeting. The next day when she returned and found out about the incident she explained that what he had wanted to print was a letter to his brother (who was in a young offenders' institution) and his social worker was visiting the family that evening prior to seeing the brother the following day.

When reading this truly painful story, we are probably all thinking that we would have asked Jamal why printing the letter was so important. But if we are implementing a behaviour strategy, and if we are busy, if others are also needing our attention, and after all there are probably 30 other pupils, it is easy to understand why that didn't happen. Seeing the whole picture can make a difference to how adults respond to situations. Had this information been known by the teacher then there might have been an understanding of why Jamal found it so hard to concentrate in the lesson, and why his reaction to not being allowed to print the letter was so extreme.

Jamal had never told anyone why he reacted in the way he did, he just blamed the teacher, who he didn't have a good relationship with anyway. As humans we all have people we warm to more than others, because of a similar interest, sense of humour or thousands of other things: there will always be those folk we get along with better than others. In this case the lesson was art, which Jamal didn't like, and there had been several previous 'run-ins' with the teacher during the lesson. Jamal was probably *less likely* to explain his reasons to this teacher than almost any other. This teacher may have been *less likely* to ask Jamal why it was so important that he went to the literacy room, and *more likely* because of past experience, to follow the behaviour policy to the letter. The support teacher knew the family situation and had supported Jamal with the letter, but hadn't realised it was required that evening.

Could things have been done differently? Maybe not, although if the teacher had asked why, or if Jamal, instead of becoming angry, had explained why, then the outcome may have been very different. Knowing the full situation would almost certainly have meant some things would have been done differently or responded to differently. Of course Jamal had some responsibility himself. But sometimes young people do not have the skills to handle situations in a way that would give them better, often much needed outcomes. Would it be reasonable to expect Jamal to volunteer the hugely emotional information about his brother being in a young offenders' institution? Think what a mix of difficult feelings he must have been sitting with. How hard that would have been for any of us, no matter what age, to articulate to someone outside the family. It was great that at least he'd confided in his support teacher, but in this scenario, the adult who needed to know simply didn't. Jamal was a vulnerable student coping with great difficulty - which sadly was compounded by these events, which in turn no doubt caused him further distress. He was the vulnerable 'child' in this situation.

So as adults, and as professionals, *we have a far greater responsibility* to respond to situations, even unexpected, extreme situations, in a way which doesn't make them worse. This means we need to make sure our responses are measured, and appropriate, and that we recognise and respond to behaviour, which is of course the means of communication often overused by troubled children and young people who, at those moments, have lost touch with (or may have never developed) any other more contained way of telling us what is important to them.

Identifying danger areas

Often in classrooms lots of incidents will trace back to a few key individuals, quite likely the pupils who are troubled, not ready to learn in that session, that day, that week or even that term. We can stand by and watch it unfold: or, as adults, we can decide to take control and intervene. Sometimes we will be able to anticipate difficulties, with a particular group, subject, or topic. If you can do so, then come up with a plan before any problem arises. It may not be needed: but in my experience, in many a de-briefing after an incident, a member of staff will express the view that they *'weren't really surprised'*. Having a plan in place to at least try using before everything goes wrong will hopefully mean the planned learning can continue for the majority, and the child or young person who is not ready to learn can be helped using specific strategies suited to their particular difficulties.

Whether or not to help pupils or students within the classroom or take them out is a judgement that needs to be made separately for each circumstance. Sometimes there is a justification for removing one individual just so that others can continue to learn. But in general, if a child or young person is to be removed from a lesson, then it's important that there are clear strategies that can be used to help the individual and re-integrate them into the classroom, although for some of course this may be a lengthy journey.

When a collision can't be averted (and there will always be some occasions where that is the case) we need individuals, adults, teams and schools to have the resilience to come up with responses that minimise the spiralling effect. I'll be looking at practical tools for this work in the next chapter. Where schools can create and nurture cultures, environments, and relationships that are supportive, then some of the detrimental and damaging impact of frequent collisions can be minimised for the class as a whole, and especially for the pupils who are troubled as well as those working with them.

IN SUMMARY

MAIN POINTS

✓ Incidents or 'collisions' often occur when a child or young person is not ready to learn.

✓ This causes disruption to the learning of the whole class.

✓ As adults we have a responsibility to ensure we don't cause or compound these collisions.

✓ Being aware of hazards and danger areas can help.

✓ When pupils or students need removing from the classroom, it is important to have planned strategies aimed at successful re-integration.

CHAPTER 6

A moment of stillness

In the last couple of chapters we have looked at how important it is to deal effectively with our emotions, and why and how some collisions occur within the classroom. In this chapter, which is very practical, I'm going to take one particular strategy and consider how it can be used by ourselves as adults, with groups or with individuals, to bring a different perspective, perhaps different behaviour and hopefully different outcomes to the often fraught situations that we as staff working in schools may find ourselves in, especially with children and young people on the troubled spectrum. My hope is that this chapter will not only get you *thinking* but get you *doing*, even if the doing is actually learning to stop for a moment: and that this in turn can make a difference in your day-to-day life in school.

Stillness, mindfulness, meditation and relaxation

In my experience, all these techniques can be of use to different people at different times, and although many people would see them as related, they are also distinct techniques. So let's begin by just considering the specifics of each one.

Stillness

This refers simply to quietness or silence, but can also mean an absence of movement. But the *practice of stillness* does not really refer to an absence of anything; instead, it's about *connectedness*, a sense of inner harmony rather than conflict. Erich Schiffmann (1996) likens it to the perfectly centred top of a spinning top where there appears to be no movement: but actually, it is moving fast but in an un-conflicted way*.

Whilst we may be spinning fast in our busy lives, many of us would recognise that there can be a sense of chaos and erratic movement in our spinning. Very often we are not fully centred or involved in what we are actually doing; we find ourselves functioning on autopilot a lot of the time, and find it hard to be present in the moment. Of course stillness is dynamic and can be present in busyness; we don't have to be actually, physically still. But it is something that needs to be practised and there are different levels that can be learned, for body, mind and spirit.

I was once asked to observe a child in class as the school were struggling with his behaviour. The class had two teachers working on a job-share basis, and they had noticed that the problems with this particular pupil usually occurred with only one of the two teachers, though generally other pupils responded well to both and were making progress with both.

The first observation went well: the teacher was young but had a quiet calm demeanour. Several times during the session she need to correct the young boy, but would approach him in an unhurried fashion, sit on a chair near him and talk in a calm, quiet way to him, making sure first that she got had his attention. When I observed a session with the other teacher, it was very different. She was also young, very energetic, used lots of gestures and was quite flamboyant. Her voice was naturally quite loud and while she was great fun, frequently laughing with the children and clapping, she exuded a kind of 'excitement'. Within minutes she had to offer some direction to the pupil I was observing, and did so from the front of the class in a warm, smiling, though quite loud, way. The child responded favourably but it was also noticeable that he was much less focussed - distracted by the general noise level within the class room, and the movement, mostly of the teacher who was moving constantly among the pupils. Before the end of the session he had been

---

* *(movingintostillness.com/book/meditation_moving_into_stillness.html).*

removed as he had become very excitable and effectively stopped working.

There was nothing wrong with either approach, but for this child the approach that seemed to involve some 'stillness' seemed to work better - even though for the majority of other pupils it seemed to make little difference (and see below p.129).

Mindfulness

The website bemindful.co.uk helpfully defines mindfulness as 'a mind-body approach to wellbeing that can help you change the way you think about experiences and reduce stress and anxiety'. I agree with this definition; to me it is about learning to be conscious of the present. So often we spend time thinking of what we are about to do, or have just done that we rarely seem to live in the moment. Through mindfulness exercises we can learn to focus on the present. The exercises are often short and can help relieve stress and anxiety, not only among adults but also among school children. It's been used effectively in business to improve performance and it's also thought to improve learning.

Being involved in the training of Designated Teachers within school and often running training for support staff I have seen this strategy used much more frequently in recent years. The testimony of staff is that not only does it help reduce stress for children but has a beneficial impact on staff and can create an increased sense of calm within the whole school.

Meditation

The Medical Dictionary Online (2016) defines meditation as

the practice of concentrated focus upon a sound, object, visualisation, the breath, movement or attention itself in order to increase awareness of the present moment to reduce stress, promote relaxation and enhance personal and spiritual growth.

medical-dictionary.thefreedictionary.com/Meditation

So this can sound a lot like mindfulness practice; and it is, in the early stages. The purpose of mindfulness is to consciously relax and focus on the here-and-now by becoming aware of the present, perhaps by focussing on our breath. These are the exact same skills that many would learn at the beginning of meditation.

But students of meditation wouldn't stop there. The main differences are that mindfulness is possible in almost any daily activity - it can be undertaken for very short times and its roots are in science and psychology - its purpose is to assist us in our daily lives and handle the struggles that our current lifestyles bring. But meditation has a place in many different religions, and the aim then is to develop a contemplative separation from our thoughts and feelings so that we can become more 'aware'. Its roots lie in a monastic tradition that in many ways seeks separation from the world, rather than support within it. There are different levels, and again it is something that needs to be practised. Both meditation and relaxation are often also linked to yoga.

Relaxation

This is simply about a process practised in order to become relaxed, but it has become a bit of a buzz word. In our busy, high pressure lives it is something that people seem to find hard to do. Relaxation is important for restoring our bodies and minds and reducing stress. We have probably all experienced the situation where we are completely tired out, have had manic days, and then finally get to where we can relax and find that our mind is bouncing all over the place. Similarly I have heard people tell me that they can sometimes feel they are constantly holding many of their muscles in a state of tension. Many different tools exist to help people relax, relaxation exercise, music, even traditional exercise.* Sometimes it's helpful to think of relaxation as being the opposite of what stresses you, and for many adults that is work. So, if you are in a physically demanding job, relaxation may be a massage, or simply lying down and listening to some music. Others of us may relax through exercise, especially if our job is sedentary. As someone working in education, with its high demand for face-to-face time, crowd control, meeting targets, sensitivity, assertiveness, diplomacy, and so on - what does relaxation mean for you? Relaxation usually reflects both a physical and mental state, and may involve attention to our breathing.

Tapping

One last perhaps less familiar technique which can be really useful in dealing not only with our feelings in the present but also emotions we may have suppressed, or other issues like phobias, self-confidence, compulsions, anger or anxiety, is tapping, also known as energy meridian or emotional freedom technique (EFT). It involves tapping with your fingertips on acupressure points around your body while also saying certain affirmations. It's rooted in what is known as neurolinguistic programming (NLP) and is easy to learn. Anyone can do it for themselves, although registered therapists can work through issues with clients by guiding them through the process. If you'd like to find out more, visit attunededucation.com and click on the tapping tab.

For the purpose of this chapter I have chosen here to look at stillness in more depth. As you can already see, there is overlap between different approaches, but I think for people who haven't practised any of these techniques, stillness is a good and straightforward place to start. Any of the techniques can be useful and are definitely worth exploring if you work, as so many of us in the school context do, in stressful situations.

Stillness at school

Many situations within schools are emotional simply because they involve humans. We are all emotional beings. As we've already seen, relationships are vital for vulnerable children: but when relationships are involved, situations can become tense precisely because we have emotionally invested in them. It is important not to see this as a

(mind.org.uk/information-support/tips-for-everyday-living/relaxation-tips/).

problem, but simply to recognise the part our emotions play in our interactions with our pupils and, as the adults involved, to learn strategies to manage those emotions effectively so that they do not add fuel to whatever fire has started up. As adults, we can role model those helpful strategies for our pupils and students. We can also teach them explicitly to groups or individuals, either as a planned part of the curriculum or when (or soon after) situations arise that make it evident such learning needs to take place.

Reading the signs

There are usually signs that the emotional heat of a situation is rising. In fact it's often easier to be aware of this in others than in ourselves. Certainly, in my experience of significant behavioural incidents, the staff who knew the children or young people well could recognise the fragility of the situation and either felt powerless to take preventative action, or found the child or young person was not able, at that particular stage, to change the way they were behaving. It is also true however that some children and young people can go from being completely calm, to entirely agitated within a very short space of time, in the way a very young toddler may go from laughter to tears in seconds.

If we are honest with ourselves and reflect on an incident afterwards, we can sometimes identify key moments when perhaps a different course of action, with a different outcome, would have been possible (*see* p.120). So often, in the classroom, we adults end up reacting to things, usually several things at once, and when we look back we realise we could have chosen a different, probably better option. But at the time, in the busyness and possible agitation of the disrupted moment, those other options were either not apparent to us or we dismissed them for some reason.

Conflicting demands

Deciding how to act when we recognise that tensions are rising is challenging. Often as staff we are trying to balance the needs of the individual with the needs of the other children. We are perhaps also thinking about the behaviour policy and its application, and the fact that maybe the child or young person concerned has specific identified needs. We may also have become sensitised to particular kinds of situations, and, if there have been several similar incidents, we may have an expectation that things may worsen quickly, which may or may not be accurate. As adults, we may be reacting to unfolding events, but equally we might be reacting to our *expectation* of what we think is going to happen as the event unfolds.

I was recently introduced to a Year 6 pupil who was on the medical needs register for anxiety, and was being educated at home. I was warned that he could be extremely challenging, given to tantrums and would throw things about and storm back to his room on the slightest provocation. On the day I went to visit him he was working with another teacher and they were completing a 'map' puzzle as part of their geography. Apparently, this pupil didn't generally take well to new people, and as soon as I entered the room he pushed his chair back from the table and stood up. While I began to chat to him, the teacher quietly put away the puzzle pieces (which were numerous and small); but the pupil then became very cross that she had put them away without him finishing, and stormed noisily upstairs.

The teacher anticipated that because someone new had arrived, the boy would find this difficult, so assumed that my arrival would be the end of the session. I can also understand that with a puzzle of many pieces it would seem easier to gather them up than run the risk of a student who was angry or agitated knocking them all over the floor. However on this occasion the student became cross because of the teacher's assumption. In fact he wanted to continue with the puzzle and was agitated that he couldn't.

We will never know how he would have reacted had she not put the puzzle away, but we know that what she expected to happen in fact did, but perhaps only because of the expectation. Perhaps on this occasion he felt he could 'cope' with the arrival of the new teacher - we won't know, although I worked with him the next week and shortly afterwards he was in fact able to work with another new teacher - a testament perhaps to the relationship of trust and security he had built up with the original teacher. On that day the decision was made hastily and for understandable reasons based on past experience. A slower pace or a moment's reflection might have changed her decision.

I appreciate that this pupil may have become angry whatever happened, and assuming that his reaction was based upon her acting upon her expectation of him, is in no way intended as a criticism of the teacher, for whom I have the utmost respect. It is simply meant to illustrate that our expectations aren't always accurate, though obviously, often they may be! Just to make it all even more difficult. So recognising that, what we need to do is to make sure that as we make our judgements in the heat of the moment, and in just a few seconds, whilst balancing lots of conflicting demands and perhaps even having different views from the other adults in the room, we also endeavour to make that judgement from a place of calm.

So as a staff team, as a whole class and as adults working with individual children, it's important that we practise whatever techniques we use to manage our feelings. We're all aware that we say and do things in the heat of the moment that we simply wouldn't say and do when we're calm. The damage is often difficult to repair and with hindsight we might often wish we had paused for a second. But it's something that can be difficult to do in an effective way when things get challenging if we haven't been practising when things are calm.

A little practice goes a long way

Staff in schools can be seen as performers. Whatever you do you usually have an audience. Lots of eyes will be watching you (and they won't all be pupils), especially when you try something new. You are likely to feel much more comfortable if you have practised. So if you haven't tried any of the techniques I described above, then pick one and give it a go. See how it makes you feel to try spending just a few minutes each morning or evening on it for a week. If it doesn't help, then try another. None of the practices listed will do any harm, and the likelihood is they will do you some good. If that is the case, then be ready to share it when you think it might help.

So if we stick with the example of stillness: as an adult working with an individual pupil, you can make the decision to 'take a moment' to be still (*see below*). Simply doing this can sometimes help get a different view of what (or what you think) is about to happen. Be explicit as to why you're doing this, without actually demanding anything of the child or young person. Simply state that you can feel your own tension rising and it will be helpful for you to just calm yourself a little and then explain what you are going to do. You can easily say that you just need a moment to take a few deep breaths, if anyone else wants to join in then that is fine, but as long as they are able to let you have that moment then that's OK.

You need to do this as soon as you sense temperatures rising. Obviously if a child has picked up a book and is about to launch it, or has another pupil in a headlock, that's not the moment to try it! When you've practised using the technique yourself in the classroom you are in a good position to try using it with pupils. It really isn't very difficult, and when working with troubled children many adults will give almost anything a try. If you aren't sure where to start, try one of the exercises over the page.

BEING STILL

- Being silent for one minute
- Sitting quietly and taking a few deep breaths for at least a minute
- Stretching and taking a few deep breaths
- Walking with the young person in silence for a few minutes
- Using specific objects - a toy for a young child to hold for example. These are often comfort items (though it can be any object): just explain that sometimes you quietly hold the item and take a few deep breaths, and concentrate on the object for a minute.
- Using prompts, particularly music or sounds, or even a favourite book or activity (simply listen to a piece of relaxing music for a couple of minutes, read or look at a book or perhaps do some colouring - they can be calming and help create a sense of stillness)
- Walking outside is often very helpful: it can create some physical distance from the place or trigger of the rising emotion. This can be done in silence or you can each 'comment' now and again on things you see or notice, sounds, sights, sensations and so on - but slowly and quietly (consciousness walking, p.138).

The idea is simply to practise harnessing our minds and bodies and bringing them under our conscious control for just a few moments. Like anything new, it needs to be rehearsed, and the first few times you try it with an individual or a group it may feel very odd. Clearly this won't work in every situation but it's worth a try - it's most effective when used regularly and can be taught explicitly and used with a whole class.

REFLECTIVE ACTIVITY

⇨ Take a minute to try one or two of the ideas above.

⇨ Note how you feel before you start and whether there is any change after the exercise.

In many schools this simply pausing for a moment of calm is something that is being tried in the inclusion (or seclusion) room first, and then, when something is found that's effective, it's tried in the classroom, maybe just with an individual pupil or with a group. Whether you are using it with a whole class, a group, or an individual, it's usually helpful at some point to give an explanation of the physical and mental changes that happen when negative emotions rise, as well as what happens when we consciously calm ourselves. Try having a discussion about the science of it: what actually happens in our bodies, how our heart rate increases and how it gets hard to listen and follow instructions: how stillness can have soothing and refreshing effects, varying the explanation depending on the age and understanding of the pupil. If you are working with an individual pupil, it's often best to start with the general and then move to the specific issues that are true for that pupil, as well as helping them recognise what's happening in different parts of their body as they begin to calm.

Dillon *was eight and had experienced a number of extremely violent and traumatic events before he was taken into care. Sadly, because of the need to separate him from his older brother, he had to move foster placements and within a few months of being taken into care found himself in a new school setting as well.*

Following a number of half-day fixed-term exclusions for aggressive outbursts where he would lash out at whoever or whatever was around, the staff who worked closely with him decided to try using some stillness exercises. They explained it was an experiment they were going to try, and had a brief lesson with the whole class about changes in our bodies when we feel angry. They then tried a whole class approach of a minute's stillness, with eyes closed, simply sitting at the desk before the first lesson began.

Staff also worked with Dillon to help him recognise the signs that he was getting angry. He was given a card with two choices: to stay in class and try the stillness routine, or to leave the classroom and go to a designated area just outside the classroom and colour in a book, something he usually found calming after an outburst. Any adult who noticed he was using his stillness exercise would simply go and join him.

There were some further exclusions, but there were a lot less: in fact in the first week after this was introduced there were none. Over time additional strategies were tried which included introducing a diary of when he used his 'stillness' to help identify potential difficulties ahead of a situation. Dillon was even heard explaining to a supply teacher that he could teach them his special stillness trick if they started to feel angry! Nothing is likely to be a magic cure, but some strategies will bring about improvements.

The benefits

The art of learning to quieten, to simply *be* in the present, is something that has been practised in many cultures for centuries. Some of the benefits are listed below. Stillness isn't really the same as relaxation or mindfulness though clearly there are links between them. It is more about making a decision to stop just for a moment so that we can make a more conscious choice about how we act. If we can learn to do that then it makes it a bit easier to -

- Recognise rising tension within our bodies, and lower it.
- Provide a mechanism individuals can use themselves after they have practised the technique (*eventually a pupil or student can clearly request time for this themselves, but please note that if they are doing it out of the class then this must be monitored and managed by the adults*).
- If you use it with a whole class, it can re-focus everyone's minds and encourage higher levels of concentration, even for those who weren't especially feeling stressed.
- If the class gets used to doing it then it can be something you suggest from time to time as a tool they can use if they feel they need to. This can be effective when adults can sense problems beginning to happen within a group.
- The stillness can provide a moment for the adults to decide where to go from there, perhaps change direction of the lesson, move certain individuals, change group compositions or switch support arrangements.

ONE MINUTE

- *Do nothing:* with your eyes open, simply do nothing for one minute, except concentrate on your breathing. Follow each breath as it goes in, feel it pass through your nose, over the back of your throat and into your chest, then out again. This sounds so easy, but when people first start out it can actually feel quite difficult. It's important to use a timer because a minute can seem like a long time at first. Like everything, it gets easier with practice.

- *Counting:* again, use a minute timer and simply count. Every time your mind wanders, start again. At first you will probably need to re-start lots of times, but this can get better as you practise. The first important stage is to recognise that your mind is wandering and practise gently pulling it back to the task, without criticism and without comment.

- *Conscious regarding:* try picking up an object and simply look at it for one minute. This is simply to draw your mind away from thoughts and into the present moment. Just look at the object, observe it, notice it, regard it. The choice of object is unimportant, although if you practise this a few times the object can become associated with stillness.

- *Conscious listening:* this is similar to the exercise above but uses the auditory sense. Again, this is not about analysing any sounds, but about learning to be in the present moment. This can be a nice exercise to try outdoors, but at first it will take effort to prevent your mind from wandering and thinking lots of thoughts. Nowadays there are a number of relaxation tracks which have birdsong or the sound of water and some pupils find them helpful; if used repeatedly, they can become associated with stillness and calm.

- It gives our pupils a chance to see first-hand that sometimes in order to manage emotions, adults are proactive. Firstly a decision is made, and then some action may need to be taken. For children and young people who often struggle on a daily basis with extreme emotions because of what's happening or what once happened at home, having anything at all to try is good, and can give them some sense of empowerment.

CONSCIOUSNESS WALKS

○ In some ways for this to be called stillness seems strange, but walking without words, even in a familiar area, can create stillness of a different type. It can be very useful when a literal distance from a situation is needed. If a pupil is walking then an adult walking with them is pretty essential at first!
Simply explain that you are going to walk together for five minutes (the time can be varied to suit the individual and situation), not saying anything at first but walking fairly slowly to restore some calm and perhaps get away from a situation. Clearly, some pupils will want to talk, and time for that can be built in, but it is important to be silent first and simply notice your body and the surroundings. If this is too tough for some of your pupils then suggest that all you talk about for a few moments is what you see, or hear. It's important not to talk about the event or tension that preceded the walk to begin with, but after a few minutes and some physical and emotional space, this might be just the time to talk about it, whilst you walk along side-by-side.

• It can create a bond within the classroom and is a good vehicle for introducing positive emotional language scripts that can be used to help yet further (*see below*) which we can aim to embed as part of the caring culture of the class.

Some more practice

There are a lot of other exercises, but these few should help make a good start. We get so used to living a life with a constant mental commentary, not just thinking but having lots of competing thoughts - a constant buzz. The purpose of these exercises is simply to try and establish some times when we can quieten that buzz. This can allow us to think more clearly, concentrate more fully and relax more.

Encouraging or introducing stillness to others

Sometimes I meet teachers who want to try some of the exercises but don't know what to say, how to go about doing it. So I've listed here some phrases that can be used. These are absolutely not designed to be prescriptive, but rather to provide a few initial ideas. Authenticity is important, so use words that are comfortable for you: our pupils and students will be unlikely to try something if they sense we feel awkward about it. The words can obviously be varied so they sound natural within the language used by the class or an individual, but the following ideas give some ideas of ways to introduce the exercises above to a child or young person, a small group of pupils or even a whole class. As with most things, it's best to become familiar with the techniques before trying to use them with others.

Start-up phrases

I don't know about you but we've learned such a lot of new things I think we need to take a moment just to let our brains be still.

I can see that some people are finding it hard to concentrate right now, so let's give ourselves a moment to re-focus.

I wonder if you are feeling a bit upset right now. Often what I find helpful is to take a moment to be still.

We all got very involved in that activity, so let's just take a moment to relax before we move on.

Maybe we should leave this for a bit and have a moment of silence/a walk/some music.

I think some people are finding it hard to settle down, so why don't we all have a few moments of stillness.

I think the best way for me to help you right now is for me just to be still for a bit.

I think maybe you are finding it difficult to concentrate on work at the moment so why don't we take a moment to re-focus ourselves.

Whatever method is used, it's often better to try something than just to let things run their course, which will usually cause damage and disruption to individuals and to learning. The examples given are not exhaustive. It is good for us as adults to remain open to learning from colleagues or others any other strategies or techniques that may help us and that we in turn can use to help our pupils.

In the next chapter, we'll look in greater depth at what lies behind the behaviour of many of the troubled pupils we work with: after all, behaviour is simply a way of communicating, perhaps when all else has failed.

IN SUMMARY

MAIN POINTS

✓ Practicing a technique like stillness, mindfulness, relaxation or meditation can be very helpful to reduce our individual stress levels.

✓ Introducing these techniques to individual children and young people may empower them to begin to take control of their own mind and emotions.

✓ Using such strategies with groups or even whole classes can sometimes reduce tension and prevent situations from escalating.

CHAPTER 7

Behind the behaviour

We've looked at some of the strategies or techniques that can be used within schools to help adults as well as pupils manage their feelings, give themselves a space to consider their next decision, and hopefully avoid or ameliorate the collisions that may occur in the classroom. In many ways what we see on the surface, the behaviour, is the tip of an 'emotional iceberg'. It's what we can see, notice or observe. The causes may be deeply hidden, but behaviour *is* a communication, and there will be something that causes a particular action to occur at a particular time.

Behaviour - why is he *doing* that?

So let's now turn our attention to what lies behind our pupils' challenging behaviour. In this chapter, I'll explore some causes and triggers, because with a greater understanding of why something may be happening, it becomes a lot easier to decide on appropriate ways of dealing with it. Even when the young person themselves, quite understandably, may have no idea where their behaviour comes from.

In school, the behaviours are what we can see: a child who objects to every reasonable request, constantly provokes other children, or shouts out in all our lessons. That's what is happening on the surface, and usually has a physical manifestation: in other words, the child is *doing* something.

Triggers

Usually there is a *trigger*, a stimulus for a behaviour to occur, which is sometimes very obvious, on other occasions may not be at all apparent. When we know particular children well, it's often possible to anticipate likely triggers for them; as we saw earlier, some circumstances make collisions more probable. In almost every class there are likely to be a small handful of pupils who find days with less structure difficult, for example: as adults we're often aware of this and will think about how to help them deal with those situations. For other pupils, we know that X (trigger) will be upsetting (having a different teacher). Or, perhaps Y is the trigger, realising they have forgotten their PE kit or lunch may cause a reaction. And a trigger needn't necessarily be a sudden or negative stimulus. Someone praising a child with a low self-esteem, who may be living with a misplaced sense of shame, can cause a disproportionate reaction that seems to appear out of the blue. In some ways a trigger can be simply anything. A few of the common ones are as follows:

Loud noises	Position within the classroom
Sudden movements	Changes of any sort
Particular smells or foods	Unexpected activities, even if they are enjoyable
Certain stories or words	
Raised voices	Distress of another child or adult
Being asked to sit or stand in a particular place	Praise for another child
	Any situation the child sees as difficult

But, if something in particular has triggered a reaction on one occasion, it's likely to do so again unless something is done differently. The old saying, about *always doing what you always do and always getting what you've always got*, really can ring true.

*The first time **Rachel** burst into almost inconsolable tears when the fire alarm was tested took everyone by surprise. Rachel was a child in care who had experienced numerous traumas. It happened a few more times before staff devised a plan where Rachel was actually taken to see how they switched on the alarm to test it. Unfortunately she reacted similarly to any sudden loud noise. Rachel had an emotional response to loud noises because it seemed that they were associated in her mind with trauma and violence.*

Identifying an individual child's triggers and then coming up with a plan in advance is generally better than 'just hoping' things will work out differently. Later I'll provide more strategies which can be used in a situation identified as potentially causing difficulty (because it has in the past), and used in advance of that situation occurring again. But for now let's consider some of the emotions that may drive particular behaviour.

Emotional drivers

We can see the behaviour, tears, tantrums, shouting, aggression, anger, or any one of numerous other actions/expressions, we recognise the potential trigger; but what we really want to know and understand are the *emotional drivers* for the behaviour, those root causes, usually emotional, that drive the child or young person to behave in a particular way given that particular trigger. Certain behaviours, like the ones in these brief case studies below leave us in no doubt about the emotional state of the pupils, even if at the time we don't know the *cause* for that emotion.

__Huian__ was only eight years old and for the two years she had been in the school, had always appeared quiet and withdrawn. In many ways staff assumed this was because of her difficulties with the language. They were shocked one day to discover numerous recent deep cuts on her arms. Not long afterwards, she was hospitalised after she attempted to slit her wrists. It turned out she was being sexually abused by an older relative living in her home.

Mayson was in Year 7, had a short attention span, and found it very hard to regulate his behaviour. When he was initially taken into care with his siblings, twin boys just a year younger, his behaviour worsened a little. However a few months later he began to wet himself with regularity in school, which caused further problems, as other children noticed. This started after he was moved to a separate foster family away from his twin siblings.

Talia was eight when she arrived from the Sudan with an older female relative. It was almost two years before Talia spoke aloud within school, most of the time staff reported that she looked simply terrified no matter how approachable staff or children tried to be with her.

The children in the case studies above were all suffering from extreme distress. They weren't able to articulate this but their behaviour gave clear indications that something was seriously wrong. These are extreme cases, but they are useful to demonstrate the point that if they can't communicate any other way, children, like adults, may articulate their emotions through their behaviour.

As we know, dealing with the behaviour, let alone the causes, can take up a lot of time, involve considerable effort and take an emotional toll on the people dealing with those behaviours. Whether it is the low-level behaviours, constantly calling out, distracting others, refusal to work or 'cheekiness', through to refusal to follow any instructions, being emotionally or physically abusive to others or having tantrums, or even more worrying situations like those in the case studies above, they all take time away from learning and are exhausting for everyone concerned.

Sometimes the behaviour is entirely within the conscious control of the child. At other times, the child is acting on a kind of impulse, either in an instinctive way or perhaps a learned way, or more usually in a way that is part instinctive and part learned. They may not be aware *why* they are doing what they're doing, they may even have determined *not* to act in that way: but somehow it happens again. Usually this is because a *subconscious motivation* makes them do certain things in certain situations (*see* p.181).

Think for a moment about a time when you have been trying to lose weight, or give up smoking or drinking, or even stop biting your nails. Making the decision to do it is relatively easy: we usually have a good reason for wanting to make such a change. Yet even when we have determined our course of action, we feel 'driven' by particular situations towards certain behaviours. So, after a healthy salad lunch, we find ourselves eating cake in the staff room or ordering a wine when we had decided to drink diet coke. It 'just seems to happen'. Sometimes it's down to habits we've developed, or associations we have made (*staff room equals cake*, for example) but often it is down to some kind of part-conscious or subconscious motivation. That other 'thought', which we may not even be aware of or that we choose to ignore, might be that we 'deserve' the cake or drink, that we'll never manage to give up, or any one of a number of other underlying attitudes, beliefs and feelings that drive our actions.

So this is certainly not something that just children and young people suffer from; we are all prone to the drives that stem from our unconscious.

***Melanie** was the member of staff who was always 'on a diet' although not terribly overweight - her size rarely changed despite her constant dieting. One day she came in announcing that she had watched a programme and realised that often she would end up eating, particularly at home, because she hated wasting food, so she'd go for second or third portions of food that couldn't be saved rather than throw it out. Staff reflected that in fact it was often Mel who would eat the last bit of cake rather than see it go to waste. Mel explained that the programme had made her realise was that she had grown up in a fairly impoverished household where it was pretty much a crime to throw out food and while she didn't consciously tell herself she needed to personally consume any and all left overs, there were definitely elements of that unconscious 'thought' in her approach to food.*

***Pippa** frustrated staff enormously. She was a very clever Year 2 child, who following a period of time in care, was in a new adoptive placement. At school she would work* *diligently but frequently destroyed or defaced her work towards the end of a lesson. Pippa's early years had been characterised by a pattern of neglect and abuse which meant she felt she was a failure, 'no good', 'never would be', and 'stupid', thoughts she would articulate on occasions. The emotional driver to destroy her work came from her solid belief that she was indeed, no good. Better to not have work that could be marked, than have work which might prove that our deepest (though possibly unconscious fears) are in fact true: or indeed find that our fears were not true, that the work was actually good, with all the challenges that contradiction would present.*

Experience

As we saw earlier in this chapter, children who have not been safe at times may develop behavioural responses to particular stimuli. A loud noise, or something unpredictable happening, may heighten their awareness and put them very quickly into a fight or flight mode. They will probably experience physical symptoms of anxiety, sweaty palms, racing pulse, hyper-alertness or even panic. This may cause them to leave their seat and seek safety in closeness to an adult or in a familiar safe place. Hopefully, within the classroom there is no tangible threat. But some children will have experienced that feeling before when there may have been a real threat, and thus will be incapable of differentiating between what *feels* real and what *was* real.

A child who has lived with domestic violence, for example, may react to loud noises, shouting, or any stimulus which reminds them of a trauma or stressful event, because quite simply, in their experience, that stimulus may mean they or someone they love gets hurt.

***Kane**, who was 10 was known to have been sexually abused by several males. He was in care and appeared to be doing well until the summer term when swimming lessons were arranged for his class. His reaction was 'off the scale' but the social worker, on delving into his notes, realised that some of the abuse had taken place on the journey home from swimming sessions.*

Think about how we feel when we do something a bit frightening, perhaps a roller coaster ride, which doesn't really pose a threat (we wouldn't go on a ride unless we thought of it as safe) or watching a really scary movie. Usually, we can enjoy the sensation of fear, precisely because we feel safe. If we really thought there was a chance the roller coaster would send us plummeting to the ground, or that scenarios in the movie may happen at any moment, I suspect we wouldn't actually go on it or watch it. In many ways, 'safe' fear is a kind of excitement, and while some of the physical sensations may be similar, the aftermath is different. We forget a roller coaster ride quite quickly, but if we have experienced a real threat it is usually something we need to talk about and seek some kind of reassurance about.

Depending on the nature of the incident, it may take us some time before we face such a scenario again. Kane's behaviour, as he literally kicked and screamed and hung onto doorways, rather than get into the minibus to go swimming, was his way of maintaining his safety; why would he put himself into a situation that in the past had been so terrible? He may not have been able to articulate *why* he was behaving in a particular way but he was giving a clear message that he didn't want to go swimming. It didn't take staff long to realise the background and support Kane who was excused from swimming, for a time, then given space to explore his fear during therapy.

Sadly children don't always get those opportunities for support and therapy. They are plunged back into the same scenario with alarming regularity. It's not surprising that they develop highly sensitive 'antennae' which, once activated by something they perceive as a potential threat, will send them spiralling into the kinds of behaviours which they think will keep them safe.

Of course as adults we know that it is not our pupil's job to keep themselves safe. That's something we expect ourselves and other adults to do. But that hasn't been what has happened for many children and young people. Imagine how you would cope if you were told to do something by someone you trusted (in Kane's case, the swimming had been arranged by his mother) only to find that you weren't safe, that in fact you endured abuse, humiliation and pain, without knowing who was to blame, without having the emotional or cognitive resources to either report what happened or to ask for help. The response that many children and young people have is to supress all their emotions. But then when faced with a scenario that *appears* similar, those buried emotions will drive their response to current events.

So as adults, we need to recognise that *the behaviour we see will have a cause*, something will be driving it. It may be past events, or the responses to those events, or it may be something much more current: but there will be a motivation, even if it is subconscious.

Learning what the particular drivers are for the behaviour for individual children and young adults is not an exact science, and often can't be done quickly. What is essential to the process is a relationship with an adult, hopefully a relationship with a person that they can grow to trust, so that someone can care enough to consider *why* the pupil or student is behaving in the particular way they do and make it their business to observe and support the child or young person as they seek to 'unpack' the reasons for the behaviour.

Trusting adults

We probably all know that it can be hard to trust when we have felt let down. A child growing up feeling generally loved and secure learns to trust adults. If adults are generally reliable and consistent, do what they say they will do and behave in appropriate ways, which keep a child safe and enable them to grow and develop, then children will approach adults with a positive view. Clearly individual differences will mean that some children are more reticent than others, some more outgoing, others more shy, but a sense of trust in adults will stand a pupil in good stead in school. We learn as we grow, if we are nurtured, that we can trust our environment. Providing we receive adequate care, there are elements of this process that we all share: in fact the different stages of our developing ability to trust were helpfully identified by psychologist Erik Erikson (1997) as specific psycho-social stages (*see also* simplypsychology.org/Erik-Erikson). Erikson saw each development stage as presenting a conflict that could be resolved through experience and relationships.

Erikson's Stages of Psychosocial Development

STAGE	AGE	CRISIS	VIRTUE
LATE ADULTHOOD	65 to death	Integrity vs despair	Wisdom
MIDDLE ADULTHOOD	40 to 64	Generativity vs stagnation	Care
YOUNG ADULTHOOD	18 to 40	Intimacy vs isolation	Love
ADOLESCENCE	12 to 18 years	Identity vs role confusion	Fidelity
SCHOOL AGE	6 to 12 years	Industry vs inferiority	Competence
PLAY AGE	3 to 5 years	Initiative vs guilt	Purpose
EARLY CHILDHOOD	18 months to 3 years	Autonomy vs shame and doubt	Will
INFANCY	Birth to 18 months	Trust vs mistrust	Hope

Looking at the early stages, it's noticeable that children develop a sense of self very early in life. Children who grow up with unreliable care from adults, through chastisements or even abuse, may develop a sense of deep shame, and guilt. It's not only trusting that becomes difficult, but will also be many other aspects of life. So often the children who have had a difficult beginning then go on to find school a very difficult place, and if they don't feel they are succeeding there it causes further feelings of inferiority. Many such pupils find it hard to establish and maintain social relationships with their peers, so they become more and more isolated or embark on inappropriate relationships. It's a pattern we see in so many of our schools.

Classrooms can be daunting places for a child who finds trusting an adult difficult because of their past experience which may have been negative, abusive, or simply inconsistent. Expected to do what adults tell them, when they don't trust adults and may not understand why they are being asked to do something, makes these pupils anxious, fearful or angry. When their general life experience may have been severely restricted in terms of stimuli, nurture, relationships and calm, loving security, they can feel really thrown when asked to do something that makes them feel yet more unsafe. Many people may have told them that school is a safe place. But *being safe* and *feeling safe* aren't always the same.

These pupils may have spent their life up to now developing strategies that seem to work for them, for example making themselves almost invisible by not responding or by avoiding eye contact with people. They may have become expert at making themselves scarce at the sound of trouble. Alternatively, they may defend themselves by getting angry, shouting and swearing, even pushing others out of the way, or making sure that whenever there is food, they get to it first. Usually pupils will only persist with these strategies *because* they have been effective before, elsewhere. For our pupils or students to find themselves in a situation where the very things that may have helped to keep them safe now land them in constant conflict and trouble, must make the classroom seem like a very alien environment indeed. The pupil who behaves in a way we find very hard to understand is simply getting by, coping with deluges of emotions in response to the stimuli in a classroom - simply trying to survive. They probably feel a sense of shame that they may have let someone down, perhaps a member of staff who they had begun to trust: or, the pupil themselves may be feeling let down by the adult, because once again they have found themselves in a situation where they didn't feel safe.

Chenice was 12 when she was taken into care following a period in hospital after a vicious attack on her and her mother by her mother's boyfriend. In the foster carer's home there was a very troubled older girl who also attacked Chenice, leaving her with a broken arm. A few weeks later when out in the town with a friend on a Saturday, both Chenice and the friend were mugged, leaving Chenice with a black eye and numerous bruises. Not long afterwards Chenice was excluded from school for what was quite a violent attack on a girl who had called her names. Chenice may have made a conscious decision that 'attack' was the best form of defence or she may have simply been acting on her subconscious emotional drive to attempt to keep herself safe. Experience had clearly taught her it was up to her to do this.

Underlying emotions

As I mentioned above, the behaviour is just what we see happening on the surface. Inside there is confusion and probably panic, and a continued sense of mistrust. If children haven't been successful in resolving this conflict before they get to school, in all likelihood they will not have had many opportunities to resolve the conflicts in the other stages that Erikson describes. So whatever chronological age the child or young person may be there is a strong likelihood that emotionally they are 'stuck' in one of these earlier stages, in essence still struggling to cope with a world that has let them down.

An emotionally robust adult will feel vulnerable after they have been emotionally hurt. The cause of the hurt may have been a betrayal, a disappointment or even a bereavement. At the very least, these experiences can leave an adult feeling fragile for a time. When we feel fragile we react in different ways, because we are individuals. When we're very stressed, and finding it hard to keep ourselves regulated, we may become 'emotionally labile': cross and angry, flying off the handle for something that wouldn't normally get under our skin, or perhaps feeling sad and distressed at the slightest provocation. And the provocation needn't be harsh - it can be the *"Don't be nice to me"* sense of fragility that we've probably all experienced. And it may take us time when we feel like this, and some nurture from friends and family, some safe times to express our hurt, and a period of adjustment, to help us get back on an even keel, all of which are based in trust - in ourselves, and in others.

These are understandable responses in a functioning, emotionally mature adult.

Imagine the intensity of feelings for a pupil who is still developing emotionally, who has probably experienced multiple emotional traumas and who quite likely has never had sufficient good relationships with appropriate adults to develop a sense of trust in the world.

When we recognise this, it doesn't seem surprising that such children and young people may sometimes seem emotional or detached: their behaviour may be unpredictable, they push against every boundary, they may not respond well even to a mild challenge. So a simple comment, perhaps to remind them that trainers aren't part of the uniform, may result in a tirade of abuse. I sometimes find it helpful to think that while they may be almost six feet tall, emotionally they are much more like a three year old, struggling to make sense of many aspects of the world and buffeted by inner turmoil. So as the adults, we need to keep reminding ourselves that *physical maturity does not denote social or emotional maturity*.

Emotional immaturity

Like other areas of development, the context of an environment that is nurturing, where needs are met by adults who are consistently caring, will best support emotional development. Physical development is best supported by experience. A child who has the opportunity to move freely and safely will develop physical skills ahead of one who doesn't - taking a child to climb and play at the park will encourage motor skills, flexibility and balance, for example. So, in the same way, a child needs an *emotional environment* that can support their development. When a child lacks physical skills, it is obvious, and the people around them realise they need support. You wouldn't let a young child climb high on a climbing frame without some degree of certainty that they could safely get down, or that you as the adult could help. The problem with a lack of emotional maturity is that it isn't always evident until children or young people find themselves in or are placed in a situation which they simply can't handle.

If a child found himself stuck up a climbing frame unable to get down, we would offer support, coach him down by explaining where to put his arms and legs, or, if necessary, offer physical support to get him down. We would do this because we would realise that he didn't have the physical maturity, skill or experience to manage the descent. The child who lacks emotional skills is very likely to get into emotional and behavioural difficulties. Though it may be much more difficult to provide the support she needs to get her out of the difficult situation her emotional immaturity may have caused, *this is the task of the adults around her.* This is our task in school.

I would hope that a pupil with a physical disability wouldn't be punished for being unable to do something when the cause was his disability. Neither, hopefully would he be put in situations that would likely lead to humiliation or repeated failure. Yet in many schools, it seems the pupils who aren't yet able to manage their behaviour, social interactions or emotions effectively are very often put in situations where they are not only bound to fail but are blamed, and possibly punished for this failure.

Rehan had an acquired brain injury following a car accident. This resulted in some cognitive impairment and other issues, such as problems with short term memory, disinhibition and significant emotional immaturity. Finding the right setting to meet his needs was difficult and eventually he was placed in a school for students with moderate learning difficulties. He agreed to go there providing that he didn't have to travel on the easy-to-spot local authority bus. In fact he was able to walk the short distance home so this was agreed.

One day however, when several staff were away with illness, it was home time and he was about to set off walking home as usual when a supply teacher demanded that he go on the bus. He objected, the teacher insisted and eventually Rehan punched the teacher. He lacked the skills to adequately explain his reasons why, was probably stressed by the conflict, and reacted in the way a much younger child might have done by hitting out - of course at 14 the consequences were greater than they would have been at five.

It is our responsibility to differentiate our approach according to our pupils' needs, difficulties and emotional state to avoid such situations developing.

Conscious behaviour and choices

When visiting schools and working with staff on issues of behaviour, I've noticed that one of the concepts that is always raised is choice - individuals *choosing* to behave in particular ways. Very often the word comes into the behaviour coaching scripts, with prompts that adults use to remind children or young people that they do have a choice. Often, clearly, this is the case: our pupils can exercise choice. But, as we have seen a little with the notion of emotional drivers or motivators - it isn't always true.

Many of us will have had the experience of having a stressful, annoying or frustrating day at work and then going home and having a row with someone, usually someone that we love, about some incidental, often fairly minor, irritation. Is that something we made a conscious decision about? Driving or walking home, did we think *"I've had an awful day today, so I know, I'll make so and so pay for this."*? I suspect not! Consciously we knew, no doubt, that we'd had an awful day. We possibly acknowledged our feelings of irritation, but we probably didn't consciously decide to get really angry about something relatively trivial with someone that we care about.

Sometimes we can acknowledge that our behaviour may be out of control - so angry, we 'see red' perhaps - though hopefully that is not a common experience for many. But although we may not generally live our lives in that way, there are probably lots of times that we don't always do what we have intended to do. We start a diet and find ourselves eating cake as I mentioned earlier, or we decide to get up earlier to do yoga, prepare a lesson, go for a run, but find ourselves lying in bed till the last possible moment. We are still in control of our behaviour, but sometimes the unconscious drivers seem to motivate us more than our conscious decisions.

So *choosing to behave in particular ways is possible, but not always, for everyone.* Imagine how you would feel if you had told everyone that you were determined to diet, not smoke or start running, then, when you ate cake, smoked a cigarette or blatantly hadn't been for a run, someone questioned you about why you had made the wrong choice, again. Yet that seems to be just what we do with children in schools! Lots of behaviour is conscious, but that doesn't mean we always make the right choice or are even able to behave in the way we have determined we will. That is us, the functioning, well-adjusted, mature adults.

Using a notion of choice with regard to behaviour can be really helpful, but it needs to be tempered by an understanding of some of the motivators for behaviour that are not entirely under conscious control, as well as a degree of nurture and compassion for those pupils who repeatedly determine to behave in one way, and find themselves behaving quite differently, often suffering the unpleasant sanctions and consequences that follow.

Nurturing parents don't generally punish their children for what are essential phases in emotional development. The two year old clinging to their parent in a new situation, a toddler saying *"No"* to almost every request, or even a full-blown tantrum, almost always in the worst possible setting. These are seen as expressions of immaturity, phases that we know children pass through. There may be certain consequences, but these are within the context of an understanding that the children are very small, emotionally and socially immature, and need support and help to develop through these phases.

Often the case with the troubled children and young people we work with is that they have not developed sufficiently to behave in the way their peers of the same age might. As adults, we always need to keep the context in mind, and remember that even when physical development may not have been impacted by their experiences, the chances are that their social and emotional development will have been.

Recently in a specialist school setting, a very angry young woman was shouting and refusing to move out of a room (which she shouldn't have been in anyway). Physically, at 14 she looked like an adult. After she had generally caused a scene, a staff member with whom she had developed a good relationship came in and said to the young woman that if she were going to tantrum like a toddler, then she would have to be treated like a toddler. The adult held out her hand to the girl. She took the adult's hand, put her thumb in her mouth and 'skipped' away with the staff member. It was funny and she had intended it to be funny (the member of staff knew her very well and hoped she would respond positively if provided with a way out), but we all recognised the truth behind it.

IN SUMMARY

▶   Behaviour is easy to see. The hard part is trying to work out what is behind it, what a troubled pupil or student is trying to communicate through their behaviour. It's a difficult task. In the next chapter we will turn our attention back to ourselves, the adults, and consider the impact that working with troubled pupils, who may exhibit challenging behaviours each and every day, may have on us as we try to develop appropriate nurturing relationships with these troubled young folk. We'll also look at how this impact can be lessened by learning to manage our stress, support each other, and work as a team.

MAIN POINTS

✓   Behaviour is communication.

✓   Certain behaviours may be triggered or stimulated by particular events.

✓   There are often deep rooted unconscious 'drivers' that motivate individuals to behave in certain ways.

✓   Usually these drivers attempt to ensure that some emotional need gets met.

✓   Our role as education professionals is to try to 'hear' the communication within the behaviour, by getting to know our pupils well and responding appropriately.

✓   An individual pupil's experience, the level of trust they can have in adults and their degree of emotional maturity will all have an impact on what triggers, motivates and underlies the behaviour.

✓   Many individuals may not always be able to make a conscious choice about their behaviour.

CHAPTER 8

The impact on adults

Working with children and young people who are troubled has many positive sides, but it can take its toll on staff. We'll look at both sides in this chapter, but I'll primarily consider ways we can look after ourselves and each other, so we can sustain our work with our pupils and students.

The highs and lows

I truly believe there is a kind of magic in observing learning. Seeing a child's face when they achieve or understand something for the first time, or watching a teenager when, after much trying, they manage to solve a particular problem, is quite simply magic. It is rewarding and fulfilling, and if your efforts as an adult in a school have helped that learning take place, well, it's all the job satisfaction a person could ever need. Working with children and young people who have experienced trouble is also rewarding, because sometimes they learn to master or at least improve skills that others have already got to grips with as much younger children. With us alongside them in school, they may be learning (often for the very first time) the kind of life and relationship skills that can make a big difference to their quality of life and their ability to function in society. Sometimes we're privileged enough to see this when we are still working with these pupils, although sometimes we might have to wait a long time to notice how much progress they've made.

But I have also worked with a lot of pupils who appear to make no progress; or, even worse, their mental health, wellbeing or learning seems to decline as they struggle to keep going. Often these pupils are not only coping with the impact of past events but, at the same time, trying to deal with present trauma: placement moves, separation from siblings, cessation of contact with families, court appearances or disrupted adoptions. But even then there may be highlights, moments of satisfaction or the reward of seeing even a tiny step in terms of progress. Times when a troubled child or young person is able to enjoy a joke with you; when they may let you comfort them for the first time; when they can remove themselves from a worsening situation without as much prompting as before; when they seem pleased to see you, despite the incident of the day before. A thousand small things can bring rewards.

> ***A few months ago*** *I was walking through our town when I was surprised to hear someone shout "Hey Miss!" I turned to see Eddie, a boy I had worked with in an alternative provision. He had a pushchair with a small child and was delighted to explain that he was now in catering college, had a flat with his girlfriend and a little boy of his own.*
>
> *He asked if I remembered what he was like at school - I assured him that I did. We chatted for a while and he confessed that he'd done a bit of 'time' for getting in a brawl, but that he was getting better now at controlling his anger. He explained that at school he would get angry, and didn't know what to do or how to cope with his feelings. I asked him what had changed. He shrugged his shoulders and said that he had just grown up; but, he added laughing, it had just taken him longer than most.*
>
> *Eddie had good reason as a child to be angry, having seen his mother beaten savagely by a boyfriend, who had also taken any implement to turn on Eddie. But somehow, over time, it appeared that he had learned to cope and in fact appeared to be in a happy relationship.*

But whilst these moments are good, maybe even inspiring, many of the adults working with pupils who are troubled experience moments, hours, days, weeks or even whole terms when the feelings are very different, and which, if not handled well, can lead to a really negative impact on the individual staff member, perhaps on their colleagues as well, and on their own families.

Exhaustion

Working with pupils who are not ready to learn can be exhausting. Regardless of the age of the child or young person, helping them is a demanding job. With young children, it may involve a lot of physical activity, bending, stretching or moving. With young people in secondary schools, sometimes we have to cover long distances, checking that they are in the right place or escorting them around large campus areas. But the physical demands of the role are often not as exhausting as the emotional ones.

Working with those who are not ready to learn often means that staff must be constantly alert and watchful. We have to keep note of the small clues that show something is going well, or not. We need to be aware of changes in mood, and make judgements or predictions about what may happen next. Alongside the children and young people, we are likely to be working in an environment of constant tension, possibly all day, every day. Conflicts are emotionally draining, but investing in relationships, which is vital when working with these pupils, takes time and effort too. Feeling exhausted when there is also a sense of success can still be difficult. But when we feel exhausted and are struggling to see any progress, exhaustion can erode our wellbeing. It is vital to make sure that we look after ourselves. This isn't a luxury or an indulgence, it is essential (*more discussion of ways of doing this on* p.170).

But just in case you're thinking that it might be a bit selfish, let's reframe that thought a little. Troubled children and young people *need* consistency. They need you to be well, and for your mental and physical and emotional health to be stable, and robust. So looking after yourself is not at all selfish; in fact, it is a requirement of the job. You need to be in the best possible place to stay strong, so you can play your part in the relational process that will bring a degree of healing to these traumatised pupils and students.

Frustration

It's always difficult to support someone and then watch that child or adolescent demolish things. Seeing a shy child build up confidence and establish relationships only to watch them being broken down by seemingly manipulative or destructive behaviour can be really hard. And then we need to support the pupil though the fall-out. This may be a normal part of working with pupils of all ages, but when we're working with children and young people who are troubled it can be a week in, week out occurrence. It's frustrating when you know, as an adult, that the student is wanting to behave in a particular way: you coach them, give them strategies to use, and then watch them do just the opposite. But the next and probably most important step is to then help them pick up the pieces, and get to a place where they can try again.

> *At only five, **Georgia** was in care and had experienced more trauma in her few short years than many adults would see in a lifetime. She was a pretty little girl with a ready smile. When she arrived at her new school, staff were all sympathetic and wanted to support her to learn how to make relationships with her peers. Initially, all went well, and she seemed to be establishing a friendship group. But then parents started contacting the school. Georgia had been pressurising each one of her 'friends' into doing things they didn't want to - giving her items from their lunch, putting hands in the toilet, showing her parts of themselves. Georgia needed to be in control. The adults who worked with Georgia felt upset at what had happened. They felt she had made such a promising start: but Georgia was behaving in the only way she knew how.*

Frustration is an inevitable part of our role in working with children like Georgia, but it can feel worse if we expect progress at a rate that can't be managed. Or progress appears to be happening, and then the child or young person takes what seems like a leap in the wrong direction. At times like these, it's easy to feel like giving up; but it's precisely then that we really need the support of our colleagues. We need people who will empathise with our challenges and struggle, who can help us find hope again, and remind us of the progress that *has* been made, even if it's not very evident at the moment.

When you get that sense of frustration, it can feel very personal. The emotions are often complex and I remember feeling that somehow I had let the child down: not only were they not making progress but perhaps I hadn't helped them enough. Support from colleagues needs to be empathic, not just cognitive. It needs to recognise the very personal way many of the adults in the situation frame the lack of progress and remind them of the truth: that it isn't their fault and that our role is confined to offering relationship, support, strategies, alternatives, the building blocks. But we can't force vulnerable children and young people into taking steps that for whatever reason they aren't able to take *at this time*.

For people whose legs work properly, taking a step and making progress is easy. But with a plaster cast on one leg, or even on both, it would be very difficult. With social and emotional damage, the 'injuries' aren't always visible but they are always present. Progress takes time, and will involve setbacks. These setbacks often happen when a child either begins to feel secure in their surroundings, or when 'therapy' starts. When a toddler falls over we pick them up, comfort them if they're hurt, and then put them back down to try again, and probably fall again. Yes, we try to remove the hazards; but we know that they do need to keep trying and that eventually they'll get there. Our troubled pupils are no different.

Sometimes, frustration comes because our expectations are perhaps a little unrealistic. If we see this as part of our own process of learning about what works with this individual pupil, it may not feel as frustrating. Learning is all about making mistakes. Troubled children and young people are often out of their comfort zone trying new ways of behaving, so there will be setbacks. If a pupil answered every question on a subject correctly, we would know that the work we were offering them wasn't challenging enough. This is true in the realm of relationship making and behaviour changing as well. Sometimes we are only reminded they are still learning by the mistakes they make. The fall-out in the playground when there had been a few days of reasonably peaceful play is very similar to a mistake in a book, perhaps in a series of addition: the concept may be grasped but not fully mastered - they can apply the new skills at times, but not yet consistently.

As Sounds-write (systematic linguistic phonics programmes) trainers we speak of a concept being in 'temporary custody': a knowledge or skill we have recently learned. If we're asked to use it in a new or different context, we can't - yet - automatically do so, and it may be temporarily lost until there is further consolidation.

> *I watched* a five year old and three year old recently and the three year old was playing with a toy the five year old wanted. He asked the three year old to swap but the younger child declined. The adult suggested that if the older one looked like he was really enjoying what he (five year old) was playing with the younger sibling would probably want to swap. Which happened, as if by magic. A few hours later however, when both children were tired the older child snatched a toy he wanted from the younger one. The five year old had learned a new tactic but was unable to use it when there was the additional 'pressure' of tiredness.

We need to be careful to provide support and familiar ground *and* allow some gentle challenge as well, but we also need to be there to pick up the pieces and help them try again, perhaps with a bit more (informed) support next time. Supporting each other to manage our frustration while we do all this, is an important part of that process. It certainly isn't easy, but I think we all know that this is a demanding job.

The demanding nature of our work

Working in a school is unquestionably demanding. Most jobs within schools require work outside school hours. A large percentage of us who work in schools also do at least some work during the holidays. Working in a school is simply not a 9-3.30pm job with great holidays, whatever the public impression may be. Lots of jobs are difficult and stressful, but working in a school with those children and young people who are not ready to learn is demanding on so many levels. It can be exhausting and frustrating as I've described above, and it can be emotional and stressful. It's precisely because children inspire us that we find ourselves back at home after work still thinking about them, taking note of something that will interest them. We spend time researching the 'conditions' or 'diagnoses' they've been labelled with, or going to conferences, reading and learning about strategies that might help. We make resources and we research, the kind of thing that people who work in schools do all the time, simply because we care and we want to help.

But that can and often does take a lot out of us. Especially with the pupils who are not ready to learn and who may well destroy the resources, be rude to us, possibly even physically aggressive. This behaviour is often directed towards the person with whom they have the developing relationship, the one they are beginning to develop an attachment to, and like any child or young person in a developing relationship, they will test it to determine where the boundaries lie and at what point rejection will happen. As adults we must never underestimate the powerful impact that acceptance can have *after* an incident of some sort. A welcome smile following an angry outburst for example; it doesn't say the behaviour was OK, but it says that there is always a fresh start and that you are not going to reject them. Saying it doesn't mean this is always easy to do: it might take a lot of our emotional reserve and we need to ensure that we find ways to refresh ourselves before and afterwards, in order to keep going.

Disempowerment

Working with pupils who have or are experiencing trouble can make lots of staff feel useless and disempowered. The staff working with Georgia (*above*), for example, blamed themselves: they thought they *'should have realised'*, that they *'should have put more safeguards in place'*, they *'should have known'* … somehow. Sometimes there are patterns, sometimes predictions can be made, but when dealing with troubled children and young people this is certainly not always the case. We adults can easily slip into feeling that when things go wrong, and the child or young person isn't making progress, we're to blame. In my experience, this is rarely the case (although we can exacerbate situations, *see* p.119-123 *on collisions*). But the thought itself (of our possible responsibility) can cause complicated feelings for the adults concerned.

Professionally it's important to de-brief and get support. We can always try something new, another approach or strategy, we can discuss with our colleagues how things could have been done differently. Crucially, blame is not going to be helpful, as staff we all need empathy and support to continue to cope with the demands of this difficult role, especially when these pupils make us often question our skills and abilities, even why we are doing the job. The other side of the issue of course is that when they do make progress, the satisfaction can be immense.

It is important to remember that it's not helpful to blame the pupil either. We don't blame toddlers for falling over: the troubled pupil is trying as much as the toddler. Georgia was pressurising other children because she was responding to her own subconscious emotional drivers (*see* p.144). Obviously developing a sense of personal responsibility and accountability is important at some stage, but when the pupil is still in the toddler phase of their social or emotional development, they are not to blame for the mistakes they make when they 'trip up'.

Finally, feelings of disempowerment as staff can also come through the decisions that we witness, decisions that maybe we disagree with but have no control over: children being moved, perhaps being returned to parents that we felt were inadequate, or separated from siblings they have attachments to. Of course we may not know all the reasons for these decisions, but watching things 'happen' to someone we care about can also take its toll and leave us feeling saddened or frustrated.

Acknowledging our level of stress

The factors above all add up to adults who are stressed. In 2000, the Health & Safety Executive found teaching to be the most stressful profession in the UK (reported in the

Guardian*). BBC news (2015) reported that 83% of teachers in a NASUWT survey experienced workplace stress and two thirds of respondents said they had considered leaving the profession in the last year. The causes of stress within school are numerous and varied, and include:

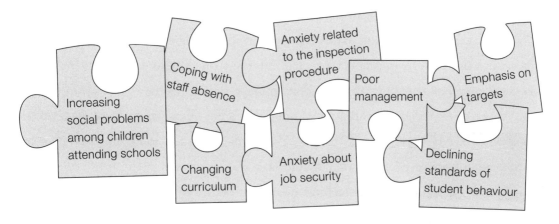

In addition to causes of stress within the school itself or related to our professional role, there can be numerous causes of personal stress.

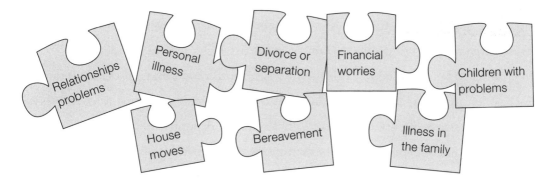

It's widely acknowledged that stress is harmful (*see* p.96). If we're asked, most of us could list at least some of the signs and symptoms, yet many of us remain reluctant to acknowledge that it is a problem for ourselves. I can only assume it's because we are still afraid we will be seen, or that we might see ourselves, as weak or inadequate in some way

* *theguardian.com/education/2011/apr/25/stess-drives-teachers-out-of-school.*

if we say that we feel stressed.

So what can we do? The first step may be for adults who work in schools to acknowledge the impact stress can have on the lives of individuals and on their families and colleagues. It's part of the lives of most school employees, and in a way perhaps that compounds the problem, in that we can too easily think, *"Well, that's just how it is and I should get on with it"*. And as we know, some stress may even be good for us. The particular work pattern in schools, times of intense stress followed by near collapse on holiday, is one that somehow means people manage to keep going. But it is not without cost. Anyone who has been working in a school for a few years will probably know some people who have been off work with stress; they may even know some staff who have left the profession because of stress; they may even secretly worry they are headed that way themselves. There may also be feelings of shame: because it's not something everyone acknowledges, people who are stressed may often hide how they feel until they reach a crisis point: *"Why can't I cope, everyone else seems to?"* or *"Why is it such a struggle, I knew this was part of the job?"*. The *"What will people think?"* fear that we are somehow weaker or less skilled than others may prevent us acknowledging the problem.

So acknowledging that stress is a reality is a first step, recognising that our feelings are valid and that they do not mean we are weak or inadequate; those feelings are nothing to be ashamed of. But then we need to do something about those feelings which, if left unchecked, will cause damage. As individuals we owe it to ourselves and our families, not to mention our work colleagues and pupils, to look after ourselves. That means making sure that we have time to eat properly, exercise, enjoy ourselves and have some kind of work-life balance, because all of these things are important. It also means being honest with ourselves that sadly, we're not superhuman! That we all have a 'tipping point' and we may be dangerously close to it by the time we realise there is a problem.

Something to think about

When was the last time you were asked how you were? Did you feel you could be honest? When was the last time you asked that of a colleague and were seeking something more than *"Oh, you know, soldiering on"* as a reply?

Stress is a physical, as well as an emotional problem. It has physical, as well as emotional, consequences. If a colleague was regularly coming into work with an obvious physical ailment they would probably be 'told' to go home. Yet when someone does eventually go off with stress, colleagues will often say that they could *'see it coming'*, and that they knew the individual was struggling. But presumably no-one was willing or able to be honest with the person, or to express their care and concern, or the individual was unwilling or unable to be honest with themselves.

Earlier I emphasised the need to develop caring cultures within our schools and it's important that the care encompasses staff as well as pupils. I am more than a little puzzled by environments that deliver 'care' to people who use a service yet fail to notice when colleagues are struggling. 'Care' is a value as well as an action, and sometimes a little care and kindness can have a big impact. It can make people feel noticed and valued, and that can be supportive in itself. But in performance-driven settings, like contemporary education, there can be an attitude that no-one should be honest; that to say we need support is to admit weakness. But acknowledging our need for support is in fact a real strength. It's also easy to assume that people have support outside the environment and of course some do, but not everyone. Knowing that change often begins with ourselves, I have found it helpful to learn to share a little of my own life; just by telling colleagues how hard something was or how frustrated I felt over a particular issue seems to open up a dialogue which is much more honest, and that in turn, paves the way for more mutual support.

Support and supervision

Having worked closely with social workers over the years, I have long admired their supervision system where there is a chance to discuss not only 'cases,' but their own responses to and feelings about the work. I remember speaking to one social worker who had gone to collect a child from a school but then had to tell the child that she was moving to a new carer. This was a decision that in fact the social worker disagreed with. The child had been devastated as the social worker had feared, and the little girl wept most of the way to the new carer. What compassionate human would not be upset by that? It's normal: it's all about empathy. But those feelings need to be identified, respected and given voice. This social worker told me that she had said to her supervisor she would need a 'double' session in her next supervision because there so much she needed to discuss.

In schools, however, if there are one-to-one sessions, they are often focussed on lesson pace, objectives, or CPD. In the high pressure and busy environment of schools, people often don't want to burden their manager, who can sometimes seem more stressed than they are!

We know the results of just carrying on as we have before: a rising number of days lost through stress, with the personal and professional consequences that may bring for the individual, their family and the school. Sadly, and shockingly, there is a rising suicide rate among teachers. So we need a different approach, rather urgently. We can't make other people change, but we can be responsible for ensuring that we take care of ourselves.

Personal stress plans

First we all need to be honest with ourselves and evaluate our own stress levels. People who experience stress, or indeed many other conditions, get used to the symptoms - we learn to live with them. Worse still, we may begin accept our symptoms as 'normal', and so the cycle often continues until there is a collapse of some sort. We are often much better at spotting the symptoms in others, so this next exercise is not about others, your colleagues, friends or managers: this is just about you. So take a bit of time, have a look at the questions below, and be really honest with yourself. See how many of these are true for you.

REFLECTIVE ACTIVITY

⇨ Do you regularly miss meals because of work?

⇨ Do you sometimes miss planned exercise sessions because of work pressure?

⇨ Do you sometimes have difficulty sleeping (or getting back to sleep if you have woken in the night) because of thoughts whirling round your brain?

⇨ Are you short tempered or tearful? (It can be helpful to ask friends or family!)

⇨ Do you often miss out on activities with family/friends because of work volume?

⇨ Sometimes when you're relaxing, do you find you are unable to stop thinking about work?

⇨ Are you drinking more than the recommended amount because it 'helps you relax'?

⇨ Are you frequently ill during school holidays?

These can all be signs of increasing stress, so if you answer *Yes* to three or more questions, then you need to consider what you can do to reduce your stress.

After becoming aware that we're getting really stressed, we need to take action, which might mean a discussion with a colleague; but then, if that doesn't help the situation improve, we need to talk to a manager. Many people seek and receive support from family or friends to cope with stress, which is good. But when the primary cause of the stress is work, some people say that they find people outside the situation don't understand. The important factor is that *you do get some support from somewhere*. This may be from a partner who takes on some of the domestic chores, or a colleague who meets you regularly for a chat and offload, or it may be a regular yoga or meditation session: it may even be some counselling or deciding to see your GP. Support means different things to different people at different times, but everyone who is stressed needs support. If you think you're too busy to look for support then you *definitely* need to make some changes!

STEPS TO TAKE IF YOU ARE STRESSED

⇨ Exercise is a great way to relieve stress, so make sure you find time for a walk or try a new sport: anything from Yoga to running, Zumba to kick boxing, perhaps with a friend or colleague if that might make you less likely to cancel

⇨ Try counting the number of hours you worked last week. If it is high - no teacher works 37 hours, but if it is regularly over 48 - then try to reduce by an hour each week until you can get it to a level where you can have more balance in your life.

⇨ If you have a work mobile - decide on a time when you will turn it off. I regularly receive emails from teachers after 10pm - it simply can't be helpful unless it is a rare emergency.

⇨ Make time each day for something nice for yourself: reading a non-work related book, listening to music, playing a game, watching a movie, chatting with a friend (not about work). If you are tempted to say you haven't time for more than three consecutive days then you are simply too busy and something will have to give - make sure it is not your health.

⇨ Be honest with yourself about stress. This really is the first step to recovery ... my name is Sheila and I'm stressed! Light hearted in this context, but not a joke.

⇨ Discuss with a colleague or friend what you find the most stressful and get some support - is it a particular class, lesson, student or colleague? Or is it the volume of tasks, or the unrealistic timescales you have been given?

⇨ Let your manager know how you are feeling.
If you find it hard to talk about, then put it in writing, and if you are not happy with the response, contact someone else, for example the union or a trusted colleague for support. Don't just let things drift.

⇨ Health is something we tend to take for granted but prolonged stress will have a negative impact on your health, so please consider more radical steps (like seeking another job) if the situation doesn't resolve.

⇨ Seek professional help by visiting a GP or clinic if you continue to feel stressed.

A team approach

When we're working with children and young people who are troubled, sometimes we create 'teams around the child', in recognition that it's neither possible nor desirable for one person alone to do this work, that any key adult requires support and that a range of professionals with different skills many be needed to help the child. And this small staff group will become stressed, especially when they're facing the stress each day of dealing with hugely traumatised pupils.

Teachers, particularly designated teachers, in addition to social workers and many others who work with children and young people will often need to read case files or histories which are very disturbing. Many years ago working in health I remember a child who witnessed the murder of his mother, another one was literally rescued from the roadside after militia had attacked his village killing his parents (not in the UK), one had been abused by four separate male relatives, and one had lost parents in a car crash and then found his grandmother (carer) dead following a heart attack. To know even a little of their histories and then work with these pupils has an impact, and so it should: after all we are giving care and compassion and trying to develop relationships with these traumatised children and young people. Just like individuals, we, the staff, will need a wider team to support us. But so often, the problem is that the whole team is stressed.

Within the entire school culture, we need to build in some time to make sure staff feel supported. Meeting times are at a premium and often meetings are of necessity task-focussed. But there still needs to be some time for staff to be supported. Individual adults, and those who make up the teams around the children, need the opportunity to say to someone supportive what the particular difficulties are and work out together what would help. Even just having the chance to explain how he, she or they are feeling: that alone can help.

I once worked with a school who were managing a couple of very young children who were immensely challenging. Following a series of fairly significant incidents I was asked to talk to the staff who worked with the individual children about strategies. Three staff were mostly responsible for these children, the class teacher, the teaching assistant and another teaching assistant who supported them at breaks. She was also 'on call' when needed in the classroom. The staff were exhausted and close to breaking point. But after just an initial discussion, and some tears, it was evident that each member of the staff team thought the others handled these children better than they did themselves. They each felt that the others managed situations more effectively than they did. This was adding to the stress levels that each individual was coping with. Recognising this in itself did not solve the problem. But an hour later there was a new sense of collaboration, and each left feeling more that they were part of a team, and feeling more supported. We discussed why it was the case that this conversation hadn't happened before. Quite simply, it was because during the day they were all too busy with the job, and by the end of the day, too exhausted to want to do anything other than seek the sanctuary of home.

This is one incident, and clearly it isn't helpful to be simplistic. But working as a team is much more effective than individuals struggling to cope alone. There can be strength and support in numbers, but there can also be immense isolation if a group of individuals are working together but do not feel they are a team.

*The '**Tour de France**' is an annual cycle race lasting 21 days and covering around 2,000 miles. It tests the rider's endurance to the limit. The riders often ride in a big 'pack', known as the Peloton, because when they are riding close together the 'drag' effect is lessened, so those in the middle of the pack will not have to work as hard to maintain their speed as those at the front. Often the best, most skilled, most likely to win riders will ride in the middle of the Peloton and be supported by their team mates so they can conserve some energy ready for a sprint finish or to gain time on a mountain leg. Furthermore, in any team, there will be a number of riders who will complete the race, every exhausting mile of it, but they are known as 'domestiques'; their main job is to support the team leaders doing*

everything from passing them water to making sure that they increase the pace to catch any
groups or riders making a break away from the main group. A team win is a victory for
everyone on the team, but while the accolades go the winner they couldn't have won without
the support of the 'domestiques'.

When we work as part of a team the important thing is the collective goal: we are working collaboratively to reach or achieve something particular. When this is the case, there will be many different roles, but each one is vital. It might not feel exciting to put the books back on the shelf in the library when a troubled pupil has thrown them on the floor ... again, but it may be just the support that a colleague needs to make sure they are not even later getting home. Making a coffee for a colleague isn't glamorous, but if they are regularly not having the time to make one because they are spending their break talking to a troubled pupil or attending meetings about the child in their non-contact time, it can be greatly appreciated and actually helps the team as a whole help the child.

Staff room cultures that are caring and supportive help adults to help students. Management structures and school organisation that can allow some time for staff to be supportive, to explore what they can do to deal with a problem, to simply swap notes on how they manage a child, to admit in a safe environment how they feel about the difficulties, can all help reduce stress among staff and make the entire team stronger and more effective.

At that same meeting I mentioned earlier, it also came out that the three members of staff felt criticised by other staff. Although the children they were working with had immense problems, they felt that other staff probably thought it was their (the staff's) own inadequacies or lack of experience that created or allowed the problems within the classroom. Supportive and caring staff cultures are not incompatible with a culture of challenge; if staff are simply not pulling their weight, or being unprofessional then challenge is needed. But beware of criticism. In this context criticism is about passing judgement, and challenge is about asking for explanation. It's the difference between saying something like,

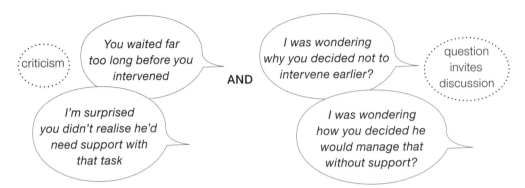

criticism: You waited far too long before you intervened

I'm surprised you didn't realise he'd need support with that task

AND

I was wondering why you decided not to intervene earlier?   question invites discussion

I was wondering how you decided he would manage that without support?

The second comment in each instance allows for the fact that there may have been a good reason for *not* intervening sooner, and that the speaker is interested to hear about what was happening for the person's perspective: the first simply passes a negative judgement.

Earlier we discussed the importance of positive language, important in our work with pupils but also important in our dealings with colleagues. Negative comments when you are already feeling exhausted, frustrated, disempowered and stressed can demolish you still further. Sadly it is often criticism that can tip a person over the edge. But challenge is important, and I've certainly been in the situation many times where I have observed that an incident develops because staff are chatting and miss the crucial moment when something could be averted.

*In a **Pupil Referral** setting recently I was surprised that the nominated worker for one of the most troubled young people seemed to be a few minutes late arriving in the classroom, so the pupil was there first and within a minute insulted several of the other young folk, meaning that break time would be tense. When it happened on the third occasion I made a point of simply asking why. Shena explained that she was also responsible for closing the external gate when the last taxi left (which was the one that delivered this student).*

A simple re-think of responsibilities changed the situation, but asking the question was

better than making a judgement that it was Shena's fault. Equally it was important not
to simply accept the lateness which was having an impact on the young person, his ability
to be ready to learn and the other students.

I hope it goes without saying that when challenge is necessary, positive language should be used and some thought should be given to when (not immediately before a lesson for example) and where (not in a corridor where everyone will hear) such discussions should take place. If we want to create cultures that are respectful and caring for pupils, they simply must be respectful and caring for the staff, and if they are not, then the very culture itself needs to be challenged (*and see* Chap 2).

There is rarely a quick fix when working with children and young people who are troubled; *but, with time and effort,* we can create an environment and culture that can support staff to support students. Sometimes that support can simply be asking how a particular child is doing that day. It shows that you know he is often hard work and you care enough to ask how he is because you know that will have an impact on the member of staff. It could be the well-chosen word, or a reassurance that it is not because our colleague is ineffective, but rather the problems are to do with the needs of the child. Maybe our colleague will need someone to cover for them while they attend a meeting about the pupil, or perhaps they need to attend some extra training.

Individual children and young people who are troubled will often establish a relationship with a particular member of staff, and it's important that they are allowed to do so. But this can cause an increased workload for that staff member, and may be emotionally draining for them as well. In some cases, it can cause friction when that member of staff can manage aspects of the pupil's behaviour that others can't, because the pupil may well be responding differently to each person.

It doesn't matter *why* the troubled young individual chose that particular person to form a relationship with, but it is good that they did. It's the attachment within the relationship that's important because they may not have experienced many consistent appropriate attachments before, and it's what we want for them because we know that when they have secure relationship, they will be better able to learn. The rest of the team however have a role in supporting that member of staff. With this particular child or young person, this adult will take a leading role. They may need relieving of some other duties; they will certainly need some emotional support and they may even need colleagues to put aside professional roles and status for a time and simply support them to support the child or young person.

They certainly need to know they are working in a culture and environment that values each individual, acknowledges the importance of relationships and can work as a team to support the 'leader', who may be one of the newest, most inexperienced, least qualified members of the team.

IN SUMMARY

MAIN POINTS

✓   Working with troubled children and young people can be exhausting, demanding, frustrating and disempowering.

✓   This can lead to high levels of stress which can have a negative impact on the individual, their family and colleagues.

✓   As staff in schools we need to be aware of the symptoms of stress in ourselves and our colleagues; be supportive of each other, and find ways to address and reduce it.

✓   Those who work intensively with troubled children and young people need a team to support them.

CHAPTER 9

Challenging our internal scripts

In Chapter 4 we looked at the importance of developing a shared language to help us communicate with both other adults and our pupils about emotions and the strategies to deal with them. This shared 'language' will also be really useful in talking with others about the 'scripts' that play in our minds. Here I'm using 'scripts' to describe the messages we give ourselves about ourselves, what we can and can't do, or even how we should feel and behave: the kind of thing we hear ourselves saying inside our own heads, or telling other people, long standing beliefs about ourselves, others and the world at large. Sometimes we're aware we hold these beliefs, but sometimes they operate at a subsconscious level. Only when we stop and really listen to the messages do we 'hear' what those beliefs are, or when we spontaneously tell others what we think and then have to acknowledge we don't know why we have that particular viewpoint.

So we'll look at scripts; what they are, where they come from and how we can challenge, refute and modify them if they're having a negative impact on our lives, or those of our pupils. It's important to recognise that the majority of us also have positive scripts, that serve us well, but here we'll be exploring limiting beliefs, and the conscious and subconscious thoughts that underpin them. And we'll consider the interplay between thoughts, words, emotions and energy, especially when these get tied up in scripts that no longer work for the pupils and students we work with, and identify how to help them develop new and more fruitful ways of thinking and behaving.

The notion of 'script' in a psychological sense was first put forward by the psychiatrist and author Dr Eric Berne (1964). In this, and in the school of therapy called

Transactional Analysis, he identified particular behaviour patterns or 'transactions', how he described social interaction between people. Analysing these transactions was a new approach to studying individuals. Prior to this, psychologists like Freud had asked individuals about themselves during therapy. Berne put forward the idea that a lot could be found out about an individual by observing and analysing how they communicated with others - their interactions/transactions - which can demonstrate or reveal the thoughts and emotions underlying or driving the behaviour. Those thoughts and accompanying emotions form the basis of what we can think of as scripts, which we 'follow' to tell us how to think, feel and behave towards ourselves and others. They arise from our experience, past emotions, memories, and the messages given to us by the adults in our lives when we were children, verbally and non-verbally.

So for example, if a child grows up with parents who argue a lot about money, or if there is stress around money, he or she may find it hard to talk about money as an adult, or always find the issue of finance uncomfortable, without exactly knowing why. Alternatively, a child may grow up in a very musical household, be given lots of opportunities and guidance, and find they excel at music performance: so their attitude to music and performance will probably be very positive, success continuing to breed success. We all know that how we think about ourselves is in part influenced by our experiences as well as responses we get from others. Our past experience may create positive as well as negative perceptions of ourselves and our abilities, often held subconsciously. Personality may play a part, but limiting perceptions and beliefs will affect all of us one way or another.

> ***Lou-Anna*** *was 14 and the only child of a single mother who was mentally ill. Her mother suffered from a range of phobias, and found going out almost impossible. She was supported by social services and the community psychiatric team and Lou-Anna attended a young carers group. But she was a bit of a loner and avoided social situations wherever possible, finding a variety of helping roles within the school*

at breaks rather than socialising.

One day in a PSHE lesson the group were discussing society and risk. Lou-Anna was an active participant, keen to put across her view that generally society was unsafe, and the only sensible approach was to assume everyone was evil and generally keep yourself to yourself.

All those years of watching her mother being afraid and possibly being told that the world is a scary place, outside is dangerous and people are a threat had clearly had an impact on Lou-Anna. Her 'script' told her to be wary and suspicious as life was full of threats and danger.

Rory was ten and came across to everyone as a bright, articulate boy who was fun to be around. But everyone noticed that Rory was convinced he would not be able to do things. Every new task was approached with trepidation, and he was convinced he would be not be able to master it. He was a particularly gifted sportsman, but even after success in several sports he was still reluctant to try a new one. If he didn't master something very quickly, he would refuse to try again.

There was a big gap between Rory and his three much older brothers who were also gifted sportsmen. He had spent much of his early years comparing himself to them and feeling quite definitely that he didn't reach the mark.

Limiting beliefs can stem from anywhere. It can be something someone said, it can be experience, particularly repeated experience, like Rory who was unable to do what his brothers could so thought himself to be pretty useless. It can be an inaccurate conclusion that a child has reached because there was no support for them to process the situation differently. A child may believes they were hit because they 'made a parent angry,' so it must be their fault, for example. Or even that it is their fault that their parent is depressed or that there is violence in the household, or that they make 'bad' things happen.

When we're growing up, we are particularly open to learning. The developing brain is using experiences and education to shape a view of the world. Limiting beliefs don't always stem from childhood experience, but childhood experience and education may give rise to limiting beliefs. So if a child grows up in a household where there is constant criticism and little praise, where efforts are ridiculed, where they are constantly put down and humiliated, then it's unsurprising that the child forms the view they are not much good at anything, that they will mess things up.

> *Marley* was six and was often in trouble at school. He was impulsive and found it hard to self-regulate. He was always 'sorry,' but then would repeat the same behaviours next time the situation arose.
>
> Due to a problem with a coach company a planned trip had to be cancelled. A decision was made to tell Marley separately from the class as staff thought he might get cross: he tended not to respond well to disappointments. When he was told Marley smacked his forehead with his hand, and said, "I've ruined it all again, haven't I?" He took some convincing that actually it wasn't his fault.

Marley happened to be a child in care. His firm belief was that he ruined things. We all know that as humans we often live up (or down) to the expectations others have us. Young people who have been excluded from school often complain that they are punished for things that others get away with, and they can't always see that if they have been the one causing disruption in the past, everyone, however unfairly, will be noticing what they do. So their perception is probably quite accurate, because they are in the spotlight in a way other pupils may not be. Of course we must always try very hard not to discriminate in this way, but unfortunately we often do when a pupil has a track record of past disruption; so we end up reinforcing the very rejection they have already experienced in their lives. Very often people behave in ways that others expect them to. When that expectation comes from within the individual themselves, they are even more likely to behave as expected.

That's why a pupil may destroy a good piece of work, may find praise hard to handle, may push the person they trust to a point where they get rejected; *because they are subconsciously constructing the situation to reinforce their own limiting beliefs which were formed in very challenging circumstances, because no-one helped them draw a different conclusion.* The 'script' they are 'working to' tells them they are no good, because that is their belief; so if they produce something that is good and are praised for it, that causes a conflict. If, instead, they scribble over it or screw it up then it's no longer good: so they've proved again they're hopeless. It sounds self-defeating - but actually it's always in an effort to keep the world predictable - a way to defend against the unbearable anxiety they've previously experienced.

So one of the reasons that it can be frustrating working with children and young people who are troubled is that so often they seem to sabotage themselves or their efforts. They're not doing it consciously: they often don't have any other way of doing things. That's also why consequences and rewards are rarely effective. If they were fully in control of what they were doing, and really making a choice to behave in a particular way, then consequences ought to be effective. But that's rarely the case. The limiting beliefs cause them to operate within a script developed in the past: the *subconscious drive* is often much more powerful that the *conscious drive* to make the right choice (*see* p.155).

Many of us are aware of the kind of negative thoughts and limiting beliefs that can influence the way we operate. They can impact our confidence, our motivation, and our ability to form relationships or develop particular skills. They may be responsible for some of our fears and phobias, they can lead to addictions and compulsions, and they can rob us of any sense of satisfaction or fulfilment. They can, and sadly sometimes do, stop people living the life they want.

Craig was almost 16 and lived with foster carers. He was crazy about motorbikes and had pictures and models of various sorts in his room and was always interested when he came across one when the family was out and about. But, notably, he never said he wanted one. For his birthday, Craig's carers bought him a session on a motorbike at a nearby training school. As soon as they arrived, Craig froze and got back in the car.

After some time and much coaxing to no avail, the carers re-arranged the session, and as they drove home asked him about what had happened. But Craig couldn't explain: he said he loved bikes, but never wanted to go on one. It was several weeks later while undergoing life story work that it came to light that when he was very young (about three), long before he had been taken into care, his then step-father had died in a motorbike accident.

Craig had both a fascination with and fear of motorbikes. He couldn't articulate why he didn't want to go on the bike, but as a young only child, his grieving mother had probably planted the idea in his mind that bikes were dangerous. Prior to his death, his step-father had also collected models of bikes which Craig had become fascinated with.

Spotting scripts and beliefs

It is the nature of limiting beliefs and scripts that they operate in our subconscious. So how can we know what they are, or identify them in the pupils we work with? Well, a good place to begin is simply with observation. Make a note of particular things that pupils do, ways of behaving, or things they say repeatedly. Pay particular attention to how they use words like *'am'* or *'am not'*, *'will'* or *'won't'*, *'can'* and *'can't'*, *'should'* or *'shouldn't'*, *'must* or *mustn't'*, *'always'* and *'never'*. Particularly when related to their own abilities. Marley in the case study on p.180, for example, thought he *'was always ruining things'*: others may say things like:

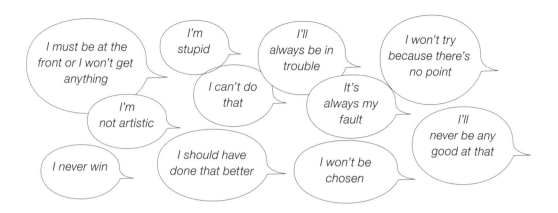

Limiting beliefs and negative scripts will have an impact on our skills and abilities. How many pupils have you come across who won't attempt a particular task, subject or sport when everyone round them can see they have the potential not only to do it but to do it well? There may be many reasons for this kind of behaviour, but undoubtedly one will be a fear of failure. Lots of teenagers and adults see themselves as simply not very creative, not good at languages, or maths, or science - because of the 'scripts' they have acquired, telling them they are no good, scripts that will usually stem back to childhood.

Internal scripts can be one of the reasons why people repeat behaviour that causes them damage: an extreme example might be someone who somehow gets her or himself into several relationships with partners who are abusive. Somehow the internal script 'pushes' the individual in the direction of such partners, perhaps believing they are all they feel they deserve and may feel 'safe' with what is familiar. We can see it in school when children or young people persistently get into relationships that are in some way exploitative; this can be particularly pronounced in areas where a gang culture predominates, though obviously there may well be other influences at work in addition to limiting beliefs.

One incident is unlikely to bring about the creation of a powerful script unless it is either very serious or traumatic, or it operates on an area that is already insecure.

More often experiences are repeated several times, and each time adds weight to the internal belief that's blossoming. It's tragically easy for a vicious circle to be created.

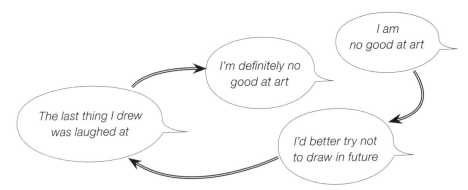

As humans we go through life testing our beliefs and seeing if they are still true, or if they hold true in this new situation. But when we have ample evidence that something is true, we'll stop testing it and accept it as reality, unless or until that belief is challenged.

The whisper

Scripts that operate in our subconscious mind will often dictate the choices we make. They will effectively tell us *"Better not"*, or *"You are no good at that"*, but when a behaviour is repeated many times it becomes the norm and there is a hardly the need even for the whisper. I expect Marley, above, rarely made a conscious decision to ruin things; he was impulsive and this often caused problems, which confirmed his belief that he 'ruined' things. His belief that he was the cause of things going wrong was so strong he even thought it was his fault the trip was cancelled. Sadly his experience of frequently being in trouble, of frequently missing out on rewards because of his behaviour, constantly reinforced this belief.

I'm sure we have all experienced some kind of internal whisper, although some people have told me that it can be less of a whisper and more of a full blown argument, as in, *"Part of me wants to do this but part of me thinks it's silly, risky or doomed to failure."* There is a difference between this kind of argument, and weighing up the pros and cons of a particular action in a rational and logical way. The latter can be a helpful tool both in decision-making and in behaviour management, when children and young people can be encouraged to think about the outcomes of different courses of action. This is more about those situations when you can't make a decision, because there is some inner conflict. Or those situations when you find yourself doing something after you had made a conscious decision that you wouldn't (*see* p.155).

In Chapter 7 where we considered motivation for behaviour, we saw that sometimes the subconscious motivator is much more powerful than the conscious. Part of the subconscious can be working really hard to make sure that certain inner (and possibly hidden) 'needs' are met. In essence, it's trying to keep us safe. When a child or young person makes a *conscious decision* to behave in a particular way, often in a coaching or mentoring session, they are acting and thinking with a degree of logic. If they get their work done, they will have five minutes of golden time, for example. Then, when they refuse to work just a few minutes later, they are probably being motivated or driven by their *internal scripts* - which will also undoubtedly have a degree of logic, perhaps a different kind of logic but logic nonetheless; *but the pupil is unlikely to be making the second decision consciously.* That's why when we ask later why they behaved as they did, in the way they said they weren't going to, they will find it hard to answer.

Effectively, at that moment, *they weren't free to make the right choice.* They were acting from much more powerful motivators than the cognitive ones which are driven by an *extrinsic reward* like golden time, or praise from an adult for 'good behaviour': but on the basis of a much deeper, *intrinsic need*, built into their 'script': perhaps the need to feel safe, perhaps to avoid rejection, perhaps to avoid failure or humiliation: or perhaps to ensure they were actually at least in part in control of what's happening when so much of their life has been out of control.

Positive scripts

Not all scripts are negative, as I mentioned above. In a positive sense there are obviously many people who are motivated to try hard, do well, and take some risks or try new experiences because of their internal beliefs and scripts. Many successful professionals have some kind of work ethic script that will motivate them to work long and hard, not always for extrinsic rewards like pay rises or promotion, but because they have an internal belief that it is the right thing to do. Positive internal scripts can drive people to try, to practise, to achieve, and to take risks. At a simple level if you are good at something and receive positive affirmation for this you will be motivated to repeat the activity. Nurturing parents of very young children do this all the time. The child builds a tower of bricks, parents smile, say well done and possibly clap: so the child will seek to do it again. It's the same 'cycle' as the one in the diagram above, only this is a *positive* feedback cycle.

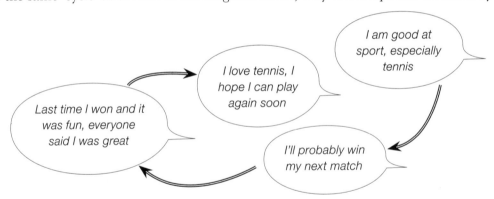

It is one of the ways in which we learn; not unlike Pavlov and his dogs. The pattern of reinforcement is important; it needs to be consistent and fairly immediate so that the reward is linked to the behaviour. And we know that the behaviour may become stronger if the reward is not given every single time. Finding those moments with troubled pupils when we can give some praise, some positive reinforcement, when so often their days are filled with negative comments and attitudes, is really important. But it is also important not to go over the top and praise every little thing; the children and young people will know immediately it isn't sincere. Sometimes it's hard to spot those small moments when praise *could* be given, when so much of the time may be taken up giving instructions like -

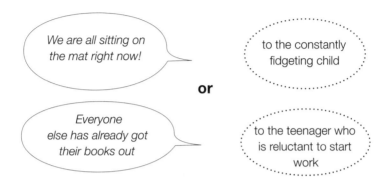

And if you work with these children and young people you will recognise this is a fairly constant feature of a lesson. But when they have complied even in part, this needs to be recognised, just casually and briefly to avoid the situation where everything is, if not negative, at least requesting action from them.

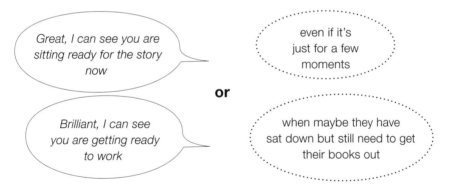

It doesn't even always need to be public, though if the exhortations to behave differently are, then maybe the recognition should be too. The aim is that slowly and gradually we can start to give alternatives to the negative limiting beliefs and scripts that are operating, in a way that our pupils won't need to sabotage.

Behaviour policies

In terms of rewards and the Pavlovian model mentioned above, other aspects may be involved as well, such as the perceived power of the individual 'rewarding' the behaviour. This may be why some pupils respond differently to the Head teacher, perhaps believing that they are the person who can make sure certain things happen. As we saw in the earlier chapter on learning, we can also learn by watching others. Assuming that an individual is able to consciously choose a particular course of action, then seeing that a detention is given if homework is not handed in on time would generally mean that the class understands the consequence: they don't all need to individually check it out by not handing in homework, though they will probably check for consistency between teachers. But for the children and young people who are not always able to make conscious choices about how they behave, this kind of learning will be unlikely to bring change.

Tyanna was 15 and her family well known to social care. She had two older sisters both of whom were or had been in prison or young offenders institutions. There was a cycle of truancy, warnings, court, followed by a spell of school attendance before the cycle began again. Tyanna was well known to the local police and had already received cautions and warnings. At school she spent a lot of time in detention or isolation for fairly persistent disruption in class.

Her mornings often began with a sanction for some uniform rule breaking. One day I was working with her at the beginning of another spell in isolation for not handing in homework and being cheeky to the teacher. As we were discussing work that needed completing, she actually produced the homework, screwed up and scruffy but nonetheless done. I asked her why she hadn't handed it to avoid the spell in isolation. She shrugged her shoulders and said it didn't matter anyway; if she hadn't been 'chucked out' for that she would have been 'chucked out for something else'.

Tyanna certainly understood what the sanctions would be for not handing in the homework, but her negative experience within school meant this didn't matter. Her internal script was negative, and considerable work would be needed to change her view. To start behaving differently would cause an internal conflict: she didn't know another way, and perhaps nor did anyone else in her family. School, or indeed any authority in Tyanna's world meant there would be sanctions and punishments. Knowing this certainly wouldn't motivate a change in behaviour. To change might even mean becoming the 'odd one out' in her family.

To summarise then; essentially, the basis of many behaviour management policies are rewards and sanctions: the *extrinsic rewards* that are offered through a behaviour policy, whether golden time or merit points, may not be as powerful as the *intrinsic rewards*, such as avoiding the internal conflict which comes from not following the behaviour patterns which the pupil has learnt to trust. These behaviour patterns may well have their roots in scripts developed to cope with the traumatic or at least inappropriate situations our pupils have found themselves in before. Children and young people who shrug their shoulders, refuse to answer or look at the floor when being told off or asked to explain their actions may not be meaning to be cheeky or insolent. They may actually be coping with a situation they find really difficult, in the only way they can. And if staff express their disappointment with a pupil because of the way they have behaved, this is likely simply to reinforce the negative view they have of themselves.

Our behaviour management policies and practices may be putting many troubled children and young people in a positon where they will rarely experience success, and actually have their negative views of themselves made even stronger. And that is neither helpful, nor fair.

Fairness

The issue of fairness is often raised in schools or indeed by parents, who sometimes feel that some children and young people are treated differently from others. How can it be 'fair' to not sanction a child for a misdemeanour, when others would be? Up to a point this is reasonable; but how can it be fair to sanction a child for behaving in a way that you acknowledge they can't control?

It can take considerable time, effort and diplomacy to ensure that behaviour policies and practices can be differentiated in a way that will meet the needs of all pupils. I can remember my daughter coming home from school one day feeling that the teachers were unfair because those who 'struggled' with work seemed to get a lot more praise than those who managed well and just got on with it. We discussed the fact that life isn't fair. It isn't fair that some children are born with disabilities, or have parents that die, or have parents who are unable to look after them, when others are born into supportive, loving, healthy, well-resourced families. The important thing is that everyone gets what they need, and that we recognise that individual needs vary from person to person. But in our schools it seems that there is too often an acceptance that *work* may need to be differentiated, but when it comes to behaviour management, some people still expect 'one size to fit all'. But it can't.

Everyone has 'internal scripts' that will have an impact on the way they behave and communicate and on how they see themselves. A behaviour policy that allows for some tailoring is essential if we are to meet the needs of these most vulnerable students. So now let's consider how to challenge these unhelpful scripts, starting with some of our own, and then looking at how we can support children and young people by helping them become aware of the damaging scripts that may play in their heads and lead them to begin to change some of them.

Challenging our scripts

It can take a while to identify scripts, so it's no surprise that sometimes even doing so within ourselves can be particularly difficult. Try the exercise below to get yourself thinking about some of the internal scripts you may have. Remember 'scripts' can be about anything: our view of food, money, work, health, other individuals: they may govern many of the activities we do each day, the way we approach almost everything.

REFLECTIVE ACTIVITY

⇨ Think of a repeated behaviour you have, maybe checking doors are locked, avoiding driving particular routes, insisting on certain rituals at home. Try to pick one that has or could easily become problematic or inconvenient. Simply ask yourself why you behave in this way, and see what thoughts come to the surface. Try challenging these assumptions by considering alternative 'truths'.

⇨ If you identify something like excessive checking of locked doors and then identify that the reason behind this is to prevent burglary, challenge the thought by asking yourself how often you have ever checked the door you just locked and found you hadn't actually locked it - usually never. So why the necessity to check? What is the worst that could happen? Often in the 'worst case-scenario' we imagine ourselves to be at fault, to be blamed, to be irresponsible, or to have failed in some way.

⇨ Then imagine or ask yourself how you would feel if you stopped yourself checking, and identify the emotion. Many people say they would feel anxious about the fact they haven't checked, worried that something awful might happen, even though rationally we can tell ourselves that it is unlikely.

⇨ Try stating to yourself a new truth: for example, *I only need to check the doors once, checking them twice doesn't mean they are more locked*: or, try checking the door and stating out loud to yourself that you have done this, and therefore don't need to do it again. Then affirm to yourself that you are choosing to just check the door once.

REFLECTIVE ACTIVITY

⇨ Alternatively, think about something you feel you aren't very good at or don't like, a practical skill, perhaps cooking, map reading, or a particular task within your school role that you never like to do, maybe introducing assembly or putting up displays. Anything where your initial response is *"I can't do that!"* or *"I'm no good at that"*. Think about your past experience of trying this skill - what were the results? It's likely you'll have had a few negative experiences, but try simply telling yourself, affirming, that it's OK to have a go at it and with time and practice you will improve. The important thing is to begin to challenge the (wrong) assumption that because you haven't been successful to date, you never will be.

⇨ Similarly it can be worth thinking about how you respond to compliments or positive attention. Many people find compliments quite hard to accept in a positive way and will jump to a defensive position of *"What, this old thing!"* or somehow try to minimise the compliment. Often this stems from a feeling of either hating attention, perhaps from previous experiences of unwarranted or unpleasant attention, or an underlying belief that you don't deserve compliments because you are not worthy in some way, not slim enough, clever enough etc. The affirmation to give yourself is simply that although you don't always feel you deserve the compliment, you can accept it without embarrassment because the fact is that you, like all of us, are worthy of compliments.

Clearly the way the script or belief can be challenged will depend on the specific nature of the belief. Where children and young people are concerned however, there are several fundamental positive beliefs that can be used to challenge negative beliefs. The list below can be a good place to start, and contains many phrases that people who work in schools may be very familiar with. It's essential to make a distinction between *behaviour* and *the individual*, and often helpful to make reference to feelings. The first is an example of what a child or young person may say and then there is an example of a gentle challenge to the expressed belief. Remember as well that beliefs can often be expressed without words, though the meaning may be just as clear: a child who tears up their work, or drawing, or a teenager who scribbles on or screws up their coursework after hours of effort - they are certainly 'saying' something.

Challenges

If there has been a specific incident where insults have been hurled or if the child or young person actually says negative things about themselves, it is helpful to refute them directly using the actual words that were spoken.

Challenging the script by using the exact phrase (repeating exactly what the child young person said themselves or what you heard someone say to them) can be very helpful, and even if it brings about a temporary negative reaction it's important to voice the truth - that every individual has value - to challenge the belief the pupil has or that they are in danger of forming through the hurtful words or actions of others or as a result of their own negative 'scripts'.

When the individual is the one who has been hurtful to others, it's still important to highlight this deeper truth.

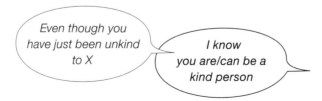

A mixture of thoughts, some springing from our unconscious mind and some being conscious thoughts, provide the background 'chatter' to our daily life. All of them will influence how we approach working with the children and young people in our care, and we need to do what we can to maximise the possibility that our approach will be constructive. So let's concentrate here on the conscious thoughts that may accompany every moment of our day.

Conscious thought

Of course we use conscious thought to guide us as mature adults through what we need and want to do each day. How we think and how well we think are skills we develop over time, and can continue to do so. However in the background of clear, logical and imaginative thinking there is another kind of thought going on, with which most of us are familiar.

This commentary will continue through much of our day. Similarly, the children and young people in our schools will be having 'thoughts'.

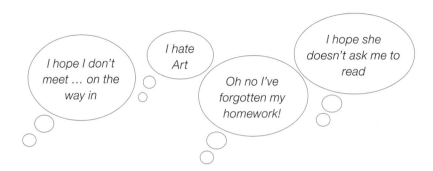

And these just give a tiny snapshot of the thoughts happening every minute of every day in our heads and in the heads of all the other people around us. Often it's tempting to think that we control our conscious thoughts but most of us have times when in fact that's very tough. We've probably all had the experience of waking in the night with our minds 'racing', often in negative spirals, and it can take considerable effort to bring such thoughts under control, if indeed we can - we've probably all lost a night's sleep at some point simply because of thoughts we couldn't control.

If I asked you *not* to think about bananas - what would be the first thought you have? Probably bananas. In fact as soon as you heard the word bananas your brain would be busy constructing thoughts about bananas. Our brains don't do well with negatives. We may have heard the word *No* or *Don't* or *Not* but the brain doesn't take seem to take notice of those easily. You may well remember a conversation you have had with someone where there is a topic you definitely want to steer clear of - yet almost certainly you will find it keeps cropping up. If you try not to think about something or talk about something the brain will carry on regardless of the *Not*. If you try not to think about something that's currently upsetting you, maybe the thought of a difficult exam, observation or meeting, or a current health concern, for example, you'll usually find it just keeps on popping up every minute that you are not actually thinking about something else.

It's also worth taking time to notice our 'automatic thoughts', and to check out whether they still really serve us, or not. Related to these everyday things they can seem unimportant, but when they are related to how we see ourselves they can have a powerful impact on many different aspects of behaviour and on our own sense of self-worth.

Our thoughts and beliefs shape our approach

So as we go through our days, being part of many situations in our schools, interacting with people, making decisions, taking action, and making judgements about what's happening, we do so with a background of both conscious and less conscious thoughts. These thoughts will 'filter' what we see and provide an interpretation of what is happening which will in turn enable us to 'choose' a particular response. That means it's of vital importance to be aware of our own beliefs about human behaviour and the behaviour of troubled children in particular. They will impact how we approach our students, what we do, and how we respond to and reframe the situations we encounter.

Aleysha worked as Teaching Assistant in an outstanding secondary school. Usually she would provide support for a whole class, in the textiles department, which she did excellently, but occasionally would have to cover in the Student Support Centre. Here other staff commented that Aleysha seemed overly strict and showed no empathy or understanding for students who might be described as vulnerable or troubled, yet was extremely patient and supportive when working in a class with students who might need support because of specific learning difficulties.

Following a training session for the pastoral department on attachment and nurture she asked if she could see me and amid a few tears, explained a little of her own background. She was the first child born to her parents who then found they couldn't have any more and adopted a boy three years her junior when he was four. Life had been good until her brother hit his teens. As is not too uncommon, the early traumas experienced by her brother seemed to rise to the surface. He caused constant conflict in the home, was frequently brought home by the police, even spent time in a young offender's institution, and throughout his adult life, had caused untold disruption to her family and constant stress for her parents. As a child herself of course she had known nothing of his background and interpreted his behaviour as attention-seeking. She frequently felt left out and overlooked as the 'good' child, and that far too much attention was paid to someone who was consistently disruptive. Understandably she experience resentment and frustration.

This had a huge bearing on the way in which she interpreted the behaviour of the disruptive but also needy students she came across. Those who were prepared to work and accept help she was glad to support, but those who were challenging or disruptive she saw simply as attention-seeking. Her experience had led her to create a subconscious belief system that disruptive behaviour was only about attention-seeking which in turn meant she was reluctant to give support to such students. During some subsequent training she began to realise some of the emotional 'needs' her brother had, and how these may have given rise to many of his behaviours.

REFLECTIVE ACTIVITY

⇨   Think about your responses to completing the following phrases. There is no right or wrong answer at this point, it's just about being honest with yourself and allowing the time to consider your responses. They may provide you with a window into some of the subconscious beliefs you may be holding.

⇨   Children and young people ...

    ... need really firm boundaries.

    ... need to know clearly when they have done wrong.

    ... should be punished when they have done wrong.

    ... need handling differently because their experience is different.

    ... should learn to take responsibility for their actions.

    ... should be treated the same or it isn't fair.

    ... often get overlooked if they behave well.

    ... get too much attention for misbehaving.

    ... need lots of nurturing and someone they can trust.

Imagine watching a school football match. One team seems to have the upper hand throughout the match but ends up losing, and perhaps some unfavorable refereeing decisions played a part. The way the match is talked about afterwards will reflect this. Imagine if the person describing the match has a view that most referees are 'biased' in some way: this view will also influence the way they talk about it and the words they use. Now let's look at how this works in situations with vulnerable children in schools where behaviour is causing a problem.

REFLECTIVE ACTIVITY

⇨ Think of a student in your school who is often in trouble for their behaviour

⇨ Try writing a brief description of the student and their behaviour

⇨ Notice the words you have used. What kind of picture do they paint of the student?

⇨ Do they give any indication about your own thoughts, beliefs and emotions concerning this student?

I often read reports about vulnerable children peppered with words like aggressive, confrontational, rude, abusive, inarticulate, manipulative, insolent … and many more besides. The people writing the reports may be trying to talk about the behaviour they have witnessed, but it can often come across as a very negative assessment. In reality, most of the vulnerable children and young people I work with are more rounded. They may display such behaviour but they may also show a sense of humour, a desire to please, and enthusiasm for certain tasks, concern for others at times, a strong sense of justice and many others things besides. We choose what we want to concentrate or comment upon.

Clearly as professionals we need to sometimes describe the behaviour of particular students, but we must be aware that our opinion and experience of them will influence the way we do that. In turn, the way we talk about or write about students will further influence not only our relationship with them but that of other professionals too.

I recently read an exclusion report about a Year 7 student who was Looked After. It described how on a particular day she had been non-compliant, insolent and defiant towards teachers from the moment she arrived in school. At break she got into an argument with some peers and she was described as being excessively verbally abusive. Later she apparently became aggressive and confrontational towards a teacher, which then culminated in her becoming destructive, pulling down displays and when asked to stop becaming violent and lashing out at the teacher.

Not happy reading: but what I knew and apparently the school did not (which was a complete failing on behalf of the adults around her) was that she had been told that morning she would be picked up from school at the end of the school day and moved to another foster care home. It doesn't change the behaviour in any way, but I suppose it would provide an alternative description - she was highly anxious, worried about moving, distressed that once again a placement had ended, she was feeling rejected and alone: once more she was feeling disempowered.

The thoughts we have about events impact how we talk about them. The way we view both the behaviour and the child will influence the way we talk. It's worth noting that we may have several scripts about behaviour as well, which will affect how we approach what our pupils do. Perhaps you were the child who was always in trouble at school, or maybe the one who would always 'dare' to do something others wouldn't. Or maybe you were the person who hated to be in trouble, maybe you hate conflict and would rather agree to almost anything to keep the peace. It's easy to just accept these 'attitudes' as simply the way we are, but our thoughts about behaviour and the accompanying scripts will impact how we respond to situations with our students and how we frame the situations we find ourselves in within school.

Behaviour is always a communication. As professionals we can choose to focus on the behaviour which sometimes we must, or we can focus on the individual child or young person and strive to understand what they are trying to communicate, or at the very least, what might be driving them to behave the way they do. If we see those children and young people we work with as problems, as challenges for and to us, that will be revealed in our communication with and about them. We looked in an earlier chapter at the importance of positive language, but as professionals we need perhaps to check our thoughts and beliefs first. Then perhaps our language will become more positive as we focus on the child and their needs, rather than on the problems their behaviour may cause.

REFLECTIVE ACTIVITY

⇨   Lester was sometimes described as a 'solid' secondary school teacher, displaying excellent subject knowledge and good classroom management. During one Maths lesson, an incident arose seemingly out of nowhere which ended up with one student being punched in the face by another. In this instance it was a Looked After child who landed the punch, and the parents of the student who was punched complained to the school.

⇨   What emotions was Lester likely to experience in relation to this event? - list as many 'likely' emotions as you can.

⇨   Lester's view was generally that students choose how they behave, and pushed for tough sanctions for the student who threw the punch. Think about the sort of words Lester might use to describe the situation and in particular the behaviour of the student who punched.

⇨   What Lester didn't know at the time was that the previous night the child who was Looked After had been in a row with another young person at the foster home he was living in and had ended up running away. He had been out all night and turned up at school unkempt and gone straight into the first lesson - Maths. The student next to him, known for his sharp tongue, had made a cruel comment about his appearance. In fact neglect was the reason for entering care, so this student had been on the receiving end of such comments most of his life.

⇨   If Lester had known this would it have changed how he described the situation? If so in what ways? Would it have changed the emotions he felt about the situation? If so, in what ways?

We may find it hard to control all our thoughts, but we can certainly control some, and how we think about our students or colleagues will impact the words we use when communicating with them and about them. Thoughts, emotions and words don't occur in isolation outside events, they are often part of the what happens. As professionals in schools we use words to explain, instruct, admonish, encourage, describe, and comfort, to name just a few, and the words we choose will be influenced by our thoughts, beliefs and emotions. In turn, they may well also influence the thoughts, beliefs and emotions of ourselves and others. It is important to recognise the scripts in ourselves, spot them in the children we work with and gently challenge them in ourselves and others within the context of nurturing, respectful relationships. Framing our thoughts about students, considering things from their perspective, looking for the reasons behind what they do will mean we talk in a different way about and to them, and that will in turn have an impact on their behaviour. As the adults, and as professionals, this is our responsibility, always.

Next in this section I'm going to look a little more closely at the links between our thoughts and emotions, before going on to consider how emotions can impact our body's energy.

Thoughts and emotions

At a very simple level, if you wanted to make yourself feel sad - what would you do? Probably think about things that you would define or categorise as sad. Do you think you could make yourself angry? If you're not sure, start thinking about situations that really make your blood boil. If it doesn't work to stir up the real sensations you associate with anger, try telling someone about those situations that really anger you, and feel what happens to your muscles, your stomach, or your face. Do you start to 'feel' the physical sensations? The thoughts alone sometimes, or at other times voicing the thoughts, can actually get us to feel an emotion. I remember hearing an actress who had played parts in several very dramatic films being interviewed and when asked how she managed to stir up tears she answered simply that she had some sad situations and memories she could bring to mind that would flood her with emotion. For many people the thoughts alone can be effective in 'creating' an emotion or feeling, and thoughts coupled with actions, like talking, even more so.

We probably all know people, who, whilst not clinically depressed, are characters whose mood we could describe as 'low', who will often see the bottle as half empty rather than half full. We probably also know some people who are much more optimistic and lighthearted; somehow when they are in a room or with other people there is likely to be more laughter and more 'upbeat' talk.

Emotions are often a response to a stimulus but our thoughts can also impact our emotions and we may 'feel' this in our bodies (*see* p.85). The way we interpret a situation will depend on our past experience, and while our brains may be doing the best they can with the information they have, these interpretations may be wrong. Aleysha, above, felt irritated by the disruptive behaviour of students because her interpretation had been they were simply attention-seeking (of course getting attention may well be a motivator for student's behaviour, because they have no other way of getting their needs met).

As situations arise we respond to the stimulus of the situation, but we also respond within the 'framework' we have for such situations. Sometimes the emotional response is matched to the interpretations we make of such events, backed up by our script, rather than the event itself, and this may need updating.

Kassie was known generally as a quiet, isolated student, and it surprised teachers that other students would often defer to her, sometimes appearing to tiptoe around her. On asking other students why this was case her tutor was surprised to be told that she had a terrible temper and if a conflict arose she 'lost the plot'. This had happened during break on her first day in the school, so others gave her a wide berth. Kassie's family at this point were all in prison following a string of violent crimes related to drugs, which was the reason behind her being in care. Her response to any form of confrontation in social situations was to 'attack,' verbally at least. That was probably the only response to conflict she had witnessed. She responded the way she did because the emotions she felt when faced with conflict 'drove' her to respond that way.

Over a period of weeks she completed some work on ways of responding to conflict, which she enjoyed exploring, at least in a cognitive sense, but she found it impossible to apply when faced with confrontation When the teacher asked her why, following another incident, she replied that she simply went onto 'autopilot'. Ways of behaving that are intertwined with earlier highly emotionally charged situations can be so tricky to change. However some months later, when Kassie had used some computer software to teach her to manage the 'stress', she found she was able to keep a bit calmer (sometimes at least) in situations of confrontation by using a breathing technique, and began to try using alternative approaches to conflict.

*Kassie learned to change the way she **thought** about conflict: then her **response to her emotions** about conflict: and was then able to change the way she **reacted** in similar conflict situations.*

Emotions and energy

When we think of energy we usually think of it in relation to either activity or exercise, for example, Will I have enough energy to do a particular task? Or in relation to the food, for example the energy in terms of calories. But energy is quite simply the building block of all matter: what we don't always realise or consciously appreciate is that we are energy. Energy is in us all and surrounds us all. And energy doesn't stay still, it's constantly on the move. Energy flows around our bodies and energy flows around the world.

In Eastern philosophies and medicine, energy within our bodies is thought to flow along 'meridians', in other words, a kind of 'energy bloodstream' within the body flowing along directional lines or channels. These invisible meridians affect every organ and physiological system that we have. Along these meridians there are also thought to be certain 'points' where the flow of energy is more accessible and can be stimulated by touch (acupressure) or needles (acupuncture). These are not new theories but have been known, documented and used in some cultures for centuries. In Japan the energy is called Ki (as in Reiki healing), the Chinese call it Chi, and in Indian Yoga it is known as Prana.

What is relatively new in our society however is the understanding that disruptions in the flow of energy can cause 'blockages'. Disruption in energy flow can be caused by traumatic events and negative thoughts and experiences. Similarly, negative emotions, distress and even physical symptoms can be caused by disruption in the energy flow within the body and the resultant 'blockages'.

So, for example, such disruptions and blockages might be created by traumatic events, for instance, being attacked by a dog. A situation like this will usually cause negative emotions like fear and anger, (as well, potentially, as physical injury) and unless these emotions are released or dealt with in some way they can cause a disruption to the flow of energy around the body. When a traumatic or distressing event occurs we may feel overwhelmed by the emotions. Our energy system attempts to cope with these but sometimes there is in effect a build-up and in some cases the system may crash - the emotions are too overwhelming to be processed so they are 'held' in our energy system. If there is a chance to deal with these soon afterwards then the energy can flow freely again. However, if not, or if there is repeated trauma, then a more permanent blockage may be created.

Many people will deal with some of these emotions by talking about them, perhaps crying, maybe feeling and expressing their anger about the situation. Others may not be quite so able to deal with them effectively and may subsequently experience or develop a fear of dogs, or numerous other 'symptoms' if the emotions are not expressed. Unlike any physical injuries which are visible and therefore obvious, emotional 'damage' can't be seen.

Developing a fear of or wariness about dogs might be quite reasonable and could be seen as protective; staying away from dogs would certainly reduce the chance of a similar incidence occurring, but would also bring many other constraints, for example, not visiting friends who have dogs, avoiding dogs in the street and so on. Although one dog did react a way that was harmful, there would be lots of dogs that wouldn't cause harm. But the disruption and blockage created by the incident which have not been processed and dealt with may remain with us, and develop into a generalised and unhelpful fear.

Of course not all feelings arise in response to previous situations - feelings arise spontaneously without any apparent cause, or arise in response to specific stimuli (hearing good or bad news for example, or having particular thought - this injection might hurt me, this date is going to be brilliant and so on): but sometimes feelings arise or are intensified by the emotions we have been unable to express or deal with effectively, which then surface in response to a similar (or not) situation.

Vulnerable children and young people will have spontaneous moods or feeling like everyone else. They have good days and not such good days. They will also respond to stimuli: a row with a carer or sibling before school, a peer calling them names, being faced with a test, or work they find difficult, or a new teacher they feel unsure about. They will almost certainly on occasions have some responses that emanate from or are exaggerated by previous situations where there have been intense emotions that have not been effectively expressed so they 'spill' out in response to another situation. The emotions that have been 'held' will not disappear but be released when anther similar, or perceived to be similar, situation occurs.

When something happens in class, the majority of the students will 'cope' without incident but a student who is vulnerable may react in a way that seems out of proportion. But they are rarely choosing freely to behave that way.

We all spend our days responding to stimuli. Feeling things and experiencing emotions in response to what is happening around us and in our lives. Dramatic or traumatic events are stimuli and often elicit a response which is loaded with powerful, negative emotions. These may be difficult to process. With troubled or vulnerable children the event may arouse similar emotions from previous events that have not been processed effectively and are 'blocking' the flow of energy, often leaving them feeling very low or even experiencing physical symptoms.

There is a growing awareness that stress or emotional issues and trauma can actually give rise to physical symptoms (van der Kolk 2014). Children and young people who have experienced the trauma of neglect, violence or abuse may experience physical 'symptoms' and may respond in all sorts of ways to what appear to be routine situations. The impact of the emotional trauma they may have suffered results in overwhelming emotions, disruption to the flow of energy around their bodies and has impact on their developing brain. People who have been traumatised will not respond to stress in the same way that others are able to, because of the trauma they have experienced.

Providing an environment and relationships where children and young people feel safe enough to express or release some of the emotions associated with their trauma, which may come to the surface in response to any one of a number of other events is vital, if they are to overcome the negative impact of the trauma.

IN SUMMARY

- ➡ Our scripts, our conscious and unconscious thoughts and beliefs affect our emotions, our responses, our energy, and our approach. We are all affected by past experience, positive and negative. It is our responsibilty as staff to become aware of and address our own 'negative script', conscious thoughts, choice of words and attitudes.

- ➡ Whatever the school behaviour policy may suggest, when you implement it with a pupil it is you as an individual who will be making the connection with the student. Your script, thoughts and beliefs will have an impact upon that interaction and the relationship you have with them.

- ➡ Once we have worked through our own negative scripts, we can begin to identify and gently challenge the negative scripts our pupils on the troubled spectrum are carrying, within the context of the safe and nurturing relationships we create for them.

MAIN POINTS

✓ We all have internal scripts that motivate some of our actions and reactions.

✓ We all have internal beliefs that give rise to these scripts

✓ Some of these may be positive but for many of our pupils, and indeed ourselves, they can be negative and life-limiting.

✓ Sometimes these beliefs and scripts prevent pupils being able to make a choice about how they behave.

✓ Behaviour policies sometimes reinforce pupils negative beliefs about themselves

✓ Learning to challenge these negative beliefs is an important step in helping a child or young person be ready and able to learn.

✓ When children or young people express negative beliefs about themselves, try to gently challenge them by acknowledging the pain in their statement, and then giving a positive truth.

✓ We also live with a stream of conscious thoughts which provide a 'background chatter' to our lives

✓ These thoughts will influence what we say and do and how we react to situations we find ourselves in.

✓ As professionals 'words' are a tool we use almost constantly - we need to be aware of the power those words can have on others and the ways in which they may react.

✓ The thoughts we have, and the words we use influence the emotions we feel and the way we respond to those emotions

✓ Emotions which have not been dealt with effectively can be 'stored' in our body's energy, causing physical, mental or emotional difficulties. These emotions need safe release within the context of empathic relationships, before we can engage our troubled pupils in more cognitive approaches.

CHAPTER 10

So, what now?

I began this book by thinking about what it means to be ready to learn, at the context in which learning takes place and at the spectrum of 'trouble' that may have an impact on an individual's readiness to learn. From there we've looked at what it means to effectively manage our own emotions and why this is important if we work with children and young people who have or are experiencing trouble and trauma.

I then looked at what I called 'collisions' within the classroom and how sometimes allowing ourselves and the individual pupil some time for 'stillness' can calm a situation or, at least, allow time to consider the next step without the heat of emotion: we then examined the impact that working with troubled or vulnerable children can have on us as adults. We explored how the use of modelling, explicit language and challenging some of the internal scripts that individuals may carry can sometimes help students learn to manage their feelings and emotions and then become ready to learn. Finally, I explored how our thoughts can interact with and influence our emotions, and even our bodily energy, and how to work with this.

How else can we use all this knowledge to help the children and young people we work with every day? In this chapter I'll describe what we can do in school to have further positive impact with those who are not yet ready to learn. I'll look at some of the objections you may meet and how to manage them. I'll re-visit all the key strategies we've discussed throughout the book, and provide more ways forward.

Relationships are central

From reading the case studies in the book so far, it's clear that children who are on the troubled spectrum have issues with relationships. They have almost certainly felt let down, abandoned, possibly abused or exploited, perhaps have never known much kindness, nurture or affection. Some simply won't have experienced any close relationships, or had their needs met with any degree of consistency, and may have only rarely felt safe and secure. They may very well not be ready to learn because their other 'needs' simply haven't been met.

So whatever other 'strategy' we use, we first we need to acknowledge that very often their greatest need is *for relationships in which they can feel safe and secure.* Building relationships can take time, effort and energy and of course in a busy 'structured' school environment, time can be a scarce commodity.

1   ALLOCATE TIME

If we work in schools we will see again and again how children and young people who are troubled can spend a lot of time and energy making sure they get what they feel they need. We've probably all worked with students who at playtime 'need to go inside' as they have a tummy pain, on the days a particular person is on duty. In more extreme situations, they may ensure they get sent out of class to work in an inclusion room or support centre, because they want to spend time with the person there.

As adults in the situation we often view this negatively - as the child trying in some way to control the situation, which is of course what they are doing: possibly consciously, possibly unconsciously, but they are making sure they get what they feel they need. What they are doing is seeking time with the person they are developing a relationship with, starting to trust, starting to feel safe with or starting to talk to. But surely if we acknowledge that developing secure relationships is what they need to do, then we need to help facilitate this.

One of the most healing things that can happen for a pupil who has experienced trouble is to experience relationships and begin to develop attachments - further information can be found in the work of Geddes (2006), Bombèr (2007, 2011, 2016) and many others. Sometimes we seem reluctant to allow time for this within the busy timetable and often intense curriculum demands within schools. Yet until children and young people feel secure and safe they will often be unable to learn or at least unable to do so consistently. So what we observe in school is that if we don't deliberately allow time for this, the individual student will 'demand' time through their behaviour. Surely it would be more sensible to schedule sessions where developing relationships is the main focus of learning *for that time*, including for otherwise well-supported children going through a particularly stressful period? It may be easier if the child or young person has been in the school for a while, because we will know who the pupil has attachments with; but ensuring that time is allowed with the key figures will help them cope with the current trauma. The adult can help them effectively manage their emotions, perhaps a far greater learning achievement in terms of becoming a healthy well-functioning adult than many other learning experiences.

ACTION PLAN

⇨   When a troubled or vulnerable child or young person is admitted into the school, or when it becomes apparent that an existing pupil is experiencing trouble, arrange times for relationship development or support.

⇨   If they are new to the school, simply identify a staff member to fulfil the role, but if you know or if it quickly becomes apparent who they are making attachments with, try to give this person time with the pupil.

⇨   The time can simply be five minutes at the beginning of morning and afternoon sessions - or it could be longer, maybe half an hour each day. It's easy to say there isn't time and we all appreciate time constraints, but as we saw in Chapter 5, *Collisions in the Classroom*, dealing with incidents can itself take considerable time and be very upsetting. It can also have extremely negative consequences for the troubled individual: exclusions, isolations, periods of not learning. If the child is looked after, exclusion can have a negative impact on the foster placement, and if the pupil is a child in need then the negative consequences could be even greater.

⇨ What to do in the sessions will depend on the particular situation. It may be a short session just reminding them of what will happen during the day and discussing any difficulties, but it could be time sharing a story or playing a game, working on a project - almost anything. It's the time spent together that's important. In some situations, time to complete particular tasks that focus on areas of difficulty can be useful - managing relationships for example, ways of asking for help, how they see themselves - schools nearly always have a lot of good resources for this type of work. It's not allocating the time or seeing this need as important and valid that often prevents us doing it, not any lack of material. *But, think relationships first, before tasks.*

⇨ Use of attachments objects can also be really useful (Bombèr 2007) and developing an 'expert' knowledge of the troubled student, for example understanding what the specific activities or times of the day are where problems may arise, and what helps and what doesn't.

2   CREATE AN APPROPRIATE PHYSICAL ENVIRONMENT

Physical environments set a context and they, together with our experiences within those environments, quickly build up associations for us. I have attended a local health and beauty setting for a massage on several occasions, which has always been relaxing and enjoyable. Now when I walk into the building I feel myself relax: it's a calm environment, relaxing music is playing, the décor is subtle but stylish, there is usually a smell of massage oil and I have my positive memories of previous massages. In many ways this familiar physical environment and my associated experiences sets me up to enjoy my next experience there. This may of course be very different for the learners we are currently focussing on who often spend their days in non-nurturing physical environments building up negative experiences.

School environments are created to facilitate learning; some are more 'fit' for that purpose than others, but space can be at a premium in a lot of schools. Often it's appropriate to conduct this relationship building work in a classroom, maybe by having a teaching assistant sit next to the young person at the beginning of the day, or lesson, or at specific points during the day. At other times it's important to have a bit of space where it's possible to calm a troubled individual, to comfort a student who is upset or to conduct the type of work that will help a student to learn to manage their emotions or to express their feelings about their situation. Organisations invest in things they think are important, which may not be, 'creating environments to work with vulnerable individuals'. But people who work directly with these learners can often see how vital a space is for this work. It may be hard to have any meaningful conversations when there are others around, or discuss things which might be upsetting. When it comes to calming someone, then the right environment is crucial, interruptions will often cause further stimuli to react to which could exacerbate the whole situation.

Many schools will have created spaces for individuals to have assistance with work, but creating a place that a troubled child can come to see as safe and nurturing may be a different kind of space, though no less important. What the particular space will look like will vary but it needs to have a sense of nurture and calm. Perhaps some comfortable seating, with some activities to hand, and perhaps the facility for playing music or space to at least stretch out in may be useful. But in many ways these are secondary: the important thing is that the school acknowledges that providing physical space to help pupils feel safe and secure and have the opportunity for interactions that can build relationships must be a priority if the school is to become committed to helping vulnerable pupils be ready to learn.

ACTION PLAN

⇨ If you are part of the pastoral team, set aside some time to discuss and plan to create a space for vulnerable learners, then discuss this with senior leaders if they are not part of that group. Maybe some space exists already but is not completely appropriate, in which case plan to adapt it so it can provide the type of physical environment that will be most conducive to relationship building.

⇨ If you are not able to exert influence on such decisions directly, determine to speak to your manager or head of department to begin the discussions about why it is worthwhile to create such space and what the advantages of doing so will be. If all else fails, see if there can be agreement to use some space for this purpose at least for a period of time and see what the impact is, and then review. You will have more leverage in discussions if you have evidence of some positive outcomes.

3   CREATE AN APPROPRIATE SOCIAL/EMOTIONAL ENVIRONMENT

The physical environment is important but so too is the social and emotional environment. Though less tangible, it can exert a powerful influence. We can probably all recall times we have been in an environment that was physically appropriate - perhaps a medical or care environment - but it may have felt hostile rather than comforting, because of the social and emotional ambience. How do people speak to you or to each other, what does their demeanour and body language communicate, does it give you permission to ask questions, to show emotion or to request support? The opposite may also be true of course, and a supportive and nurturing social and emotional environment can sometimes mitigate the negative impact of a poor physical environment.

We discussed the importance of the organisational culture in Chapter 2: creating an appropriate social and emotional environment can take time and effort. It begins with a willingness to change (if it isn't currently supportive or nurturing) and a starting point may be the value or mission statements. But they don't *create* the right environment by themselves. It is how they are interpreted and delivered that will make the difference.

ACTION PLAN

⇨ As adults we are in the school environment. We might contribute to it but we will also be experiencing it. So, as a member of staff, you'll have an opinion, but it might not be the same as sitting in a class as a student, particularly as a vulnerable student. *Learning walks* have become an acceptable way of observing behaviour and the general 'feel' of a school environment. This can be a great way to start. Pastoral staff could go on learning walks as well, but the emphasis would be on observing and reporting on the social and emotional environment they witness.

⇨ What is the tone of the conversations between staff and students, between staff, between students? What language is used if students are being guided or directed? What is the response when they request help?

⇨ What do children and young people say if you ask them about the social and emotional environment of the school? How do they feel at school? Do they feel they can ask for help? Do they know who can they go to, if they have problems? And so on.

⇨ Once completed by more than one person, a discussion can begin. Some schools have a few staff who could be described as authoritarian and have that kind of approach to behaviour management. Change is tough and there need to be both clear **reasons** for it - *(such behavioural approaches are rarely effective with vulnerable or troubled children)* and a **benefit** *(other approaches will be more effective, making the class easier to manage and the job more rewarding for the individual)*. Hearing this kind of message initially from someone outside the organisation can be a good way to begin such discussions.

4   LEARN AND USE A SHARED LANGUAGE

In Chapters 4 and 9 we looked at language, at the power words can have and at how important it is to be able to talk about emotions and give positive messages to vulnerable children and young people, in part to counter their negative self-beliefs and internal chatter. What is said is important. But it is not just what is said. What are the other messages? What is displayed? How does the behaviour policy convey the message that every individual is valued even if their behaviour can be problematic at times?

I'm sure almost everyone will have had the experience of saying the wrong thing, perhaps using a swear word in an environment where you wouldn't usually or using the name of a friend's 'ex' rather than their current partner. You don't intend to do it, but it sort of falls out of your mouth. Usually we're in control of our speech. However we're all humans and we all make mistakes *or* slip into bad habits where our language can become negative. Negative language has a negative impact that may be far greater than we realise.

Just this week in the paper there was a story of a girl at a school who had been given a certificate for being the person most likely to be on the Jeremy Kyle show! She wasn't happy about this, as you can imagine, any more than you or I would be. I will let you ponder yourself what message this might have given. Clearly humour is an important part of school life, but the joke must be funny for everyone. Close friends may take liberties, but people in positions of power need to exercise care.

ACTION PLAN

⇨   Conduct a message audit. Look at the words that are used or displayed in the school - what message do they convey? In one setting where I worked, following an inset session on using positive language, staff were asked to record themselves (just an audio recording) interacting with a student or teaching a lesson for a maximum of 30 minutes.
Quite a long time, in fact long enough to forget they were recording themselves! The next step was to listen to the recording (fairly non-threatening), and note the number of times language was negative - saying *Don't, Stop,* or *Not that* and so on. It was an illuminating exercise and one that was the start of a much longer period where language was a focus for the whole setting. You might like to try it yourself.

5   BEHAVIOUR POLICIES/INCLUSION/EXCLUSION

Exclusion, whether to home, another setting or elsewhere within the school sends a message to the student concerned as well as to the other students and staff. The message it is designed to send is that certain behaviours will not be tolerated. Of course it communicates a lot of other messages as well, of rejection and failure for example. It may well worsen already difficult relationships with peers or teachers, and it often removes children from the learning environment. The exclusion itself actually achieves nothing positive for the student (if it did, each student would only be excluded once, and then change their behaviour) though it might achieve something positive for others, a cooling off period, or a calmer classroom and so on. We need to remember that time away from the classroom can be really positive if something is done during that time that actually helps the student, in an environment conducive to learning. Sitting in a bare 'corale' facing an empty wall and being told to be quiet is unlikely to achieve a positive outcome.

Reviewing policies is almost always a good thing. Reviewing them with a view to how the troubled student will 'experience' that policy is vital. Please bear in mind as you do so that troubled students are likely to be:

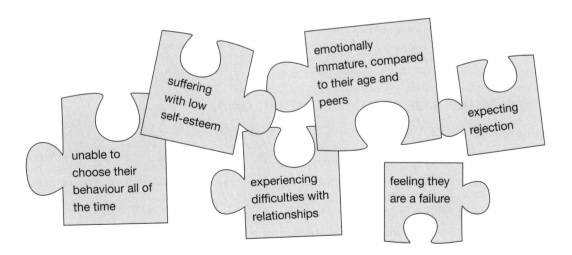

In addition, if a child or young person is looked after, then an exclusion to home or a reduced timetable is likely to put pressure on the placement and the student may experience the rejection of a placement breakdown. What alternatives to total exclusion might there be? Some schools have tried excluding to another of their sites, or to a designated highly supported area in the school.

ACTION PLAN

⇨ First review the behaviour policy of the setting through the lens of a troubled child or young person. Consider the impact of the current policies and their implementation. Then consider how the policies can create **opportunities** for the support they need to be given. This may be time with their attachment figure, work on labelling and expressing emotions with staff who are comfortable teaching this, or teaching specific strategies to help them manage more effectively the situations that have led to the incidents occurring.

⇨ We seem able to see 'differentiation' as essential for learning needs, but unless social and emotional needs can also be met with a differentiated approach, the troubled student is unlikely to be ready to learn. Think of it and explain it to others in terms of different needs. There'd be no problem in providing resources in large print for a student with sight problems - people would be unlikely to say that wasn't fair!

⇨ Most fixed term exclusions happen for persistent disruption. So if it keeps happening after the first exclusion then clearly another approach is needed. Incident analysis can help staff work out when and why such incidents occur, and identify more appropriate and effective interventions to minimise them.

---

6   PRIORITISE TIME TO DEVELOP STRATEGIES

Training time for staff within schools is always at a premium. Often as a Head of a Virtual School I am asked to deliver training for staff in schools, the need has been identified and the will is there. Sadly however identifying a date when this training can be delivered sometimes pushes it back for months. A shift in perspective is needed. Ensuring lessons are good and meeting the learning and curriculum needs of the students is clearly a priority: but for pupils who aren't ready to learn neither may have much impact, and if those pupils are disrupting the learning of others then it may be time to reassess priorities within the school.

Again as a Head of a Virtual school I often organise and deliver training for Designated Teachers and Special Educational Needs Co-ordinators, and it's important to ensure that they and the teams they work with are knowledgeable and skilled. The frustration is sometimes that at such events it is like preaching to the converted. It may be the newly qualitied teacher, long-established staff or members of the senior leadership team who have a greater need for the training.

It causes problems for our troubled pupils if some staff seem to understand their needs, emotions and struggles, and others simply keep on admonishing them for behaviours they aren't yet in control of, and emotions and feelings they can't yet express appropriately. We need to provide consistency.

ACTION PLAN

⇨   Spend some time identifying the training priorities you see are needed within the staff as a whole. This is likely to include some knowledge-based training, on why vulnerable learners behave the way they do, and also some skills training. Learning new skills takes time, but as we've seen, staff dealing with these students need to be able to manage their own feelings and emotions effectively and develop ways of being able to talk comfortably about them with their pupils. As we've also seen, pupils are likely to learn best when we, the staff, feel comfortable and safe in our own learning. If a session is delivered at the end of a long day when people are worrying about all the work they have to do then it's unlikely they will have time and space to really benefit from it. So please plan accordingly.

⇨   As a school, some of the strategies can be further developed - as discussed in Chapter 6 for example. The end point is to ensure each and every member of staff is equipped with a 'bag' of strategies they can use with these vulnerable learners. Working as a whole team will provide the level of consistency that will allow the strategies to be as effective as possible. The likelihood is that schools have some of these strategies already in place and in use, but in might be they are in small 'pockets' of expertise, and wider sharing and employment of them could bring benefit to many more learners.

7 SUPERVISION AND SUPPORT

If staff are to commit to helping students with the needs and emotions which are preventing them being ready to learn, it will create a challenge for some more than others. Supporting staff is not an optional extra. All our vulnerable learners need consistency and need the relationships they develop with staff. And supporting staff is a vital part of supporting vulnerable learners. As we discussed earlier, the supervision model isn't widely used within schools, but that doesn't mean it can't be. There are numerous ways this can be developed in a school so it can be incorporated in a way that suits the particular school. But, it's critical it is not done 'secretly'; its importance needs to be visible to others, even if they may not initially recognise its value.

Such practice may begin with setting aside part of a regular team meeting to share difficulties that are being experienced as a group, or using that time to offer support to particular individuals, especially those who have to spend a lot of time each day dealing with those who are troubled or vulnerable. It could also be more structured and embedded into the school management structure. Whole staff meetings could begin with time being set aside for staff to seek support from other member of the staff team.

ACTION PLAN

⇨ I'm not always a fan of surveys, but try asking staff (in any way you devise) if they would value a regular opportunity to discuss issues they are facing with pupils and how they would like that to happen. Presenting the leaders of the school with the views of the whole staff or a significant number may build a stronger case than just saying that you as an individual believe this is necessary. In my experience if people want something they can often be very creative about how it could be fitted in to already packed days.

⇨ Another idea is to start drop-in sessions as a designated teacher, special educational needs co-ordinator or member of the inclusion or pastoral team - for other members of staff. This will again simply provide time when staff members can come and discuss either particular students, or approaches, or even issues they have personally in dealing with the vulnerable learners. It's not the same as regular supportive supervision slots with managers who understand the needs of the pupils and the challenges they can create for staff, but at least it can be one way that individual staff can be supported.

8   PUSH AND CHALLENGE ARE ESSENTIAL

It's vital that we challenge the implementation of existing practices and policies if it is evident that they detract from the learning journey of the troubled and vulnerable learners, or they are causing frustrations and exhaustion for the staff working with them. Staff may need support to formulate the challenge and propose solutions.

It's only right that we all want to see vulnerable learners dealt with in a way that respects them as individuals, acknowledges the difficulties they have or are experiencing and will allow them to move forward rather than damaging them further. It is also OK to feel angry when this doesn't happen, through lack of knowledge or skills, and shout to our managers (metaphorically!) that it isn't fair or just or right. If we want to change something, sometimes we have to fight for it. Malcolm X, Gandhi, the suffragettes and many others saw situations that weren't right or just and decided *not* to accept them, but rather to challenge the status quo, often at great personal cost. But that is how change comes about.

What I hear from staff in schools I visit is that sometimes school leaders don't listen. No-one can be responsible for the actions and attitudes of others, but we can all be responsible for challenging situations, and the individuals within those situations, and hold them to account. It might be uncomfortable, it might not help our relationships with senior leaders for a time, but so long as we are non-blaming, inclusive in our approach and persistent, it may be one step on the pathway to improving the experience of the troubled and vulnerable pupils in our schools.

Perhaps not just within our schools. When we witness looked after children and young people moving placements numerous times, we should challenge this. When we see key people in their lives not attending meetings, we should challenge them. When we see decisions being taken that we genuinely feel will hinder or damage a young person rather than help, we should challenge them. If professionals are not sharing information which would have an impact on how a learner may be managed within a school, it should be challenged.

This challenge can be given professionally and politely but it should be given. It can be directed to people within the school, to local authorities or to private or voluntary agencies who have responsibility. It could even be directed to councillors or MPs. But without challenge things are unlikely to improve.

ACTION PLAN

⇨ With the support of a team, discuss the things you have witnessed in the past that have been unhelpful or damaging. It could simply be individual comments or it could be the impact of particular policies within the school. But also consider how things could be done differently - don't just identify the problem, but be prepared to offer a solution as well.

⇨ Then consider how best to deliver a challenge in the future. It may be hard, but not impossible, and it needs the right forum to discuss past events. Often it might be simply picking up on instances of negative language and suggesting an alternative - which could then be put on posters and displayed in particular areas. Or it could be reviewing policies or practices and considering how these could be changed to achieve better outcomes for the learners you work with. This may not bring instant change, but by highlighting several instances and thinking them through together, it can often begin the dialogue.

Counting the cost

Beginning to get things right for vulnerable learners and helping them to become ready to learn will have a cost. It will need time, which in staffing terms, is often a cost. Creating the right environment, gathering resources and providing staff training all have a cost. But there is *also* a cost to *not* getting it right, not developing those skills and strategies, polices and environments that would make a difference to troubled individuals. It is a much harder cost to count.

Within schools it may be disrupted lessons, the time needed to 'mop up' after collisions, it may mean the cost of staff leaving, worn out by their responsibilities, and there may be personal costs to the adults involved in terms of stress which of course can have a negative impact on their own health and relationships.

For our vulnerable learners, the costs may be far greater. The educational outcomes for children in care are well below their peers at every key stage (DFE 2015). That doesn't take account of the human distress of an increased likelihood of abusing substances, of committing crime, of finding relationships hard, of experiencing violence, of experiencing mental illness, even to having their own children taken into care. These costs are far too high for the individual, as well as too high for society. Which effectively means all of us.

Some funding is available through pupil premium at the moment. The remit for the Looked After Children's pupil premium grant is that it should be used on things that will improve educational outcomes. Work which ensures that they can become ready to learn, perhaps only in short bursts initially, would be a wise use of this funding. Of course it isn't available for every learner on the spectrum of trouble. But the cost of *not* allocating money, resources and time to these learners could end up being even higher, both financially and in terms of human distress and misery. Let's do everything we can together to turn the tide and make a difference.

IN SUMMARY

I have been privileged in my work as a nurse, health visitor, teacher, SENCo, Inclusion officer and as Head of and within Virtual Schools for children in care to witness a number of amazing professionals at work with children and young people who could be aptly described as troubled or vulnerable. Within schools and colleges such staff are sometimes the lone voice advocating on behalf of these learners - who often are not ready, or in a place where they can learn.

- These are the professionals, whether teachers, teaching assistants, learning support assistants, mentors, after-school club workers, SEN workers, receptionists or school leaders or Head teachers who will go home and find themselves thinking of other ways they might support those who aren't able to learn or even survive emotionally within the school environment. Much of this book is based on the discussions I've had with such staff, either focussing on individual students or during the more general training I have delivered; and of course on my own experience of both direct and indirect work with such students.

- The purpose of the book is to encourage, equip and challenge. To encourage those who are already working with troubled pupils, maybe feeling quite isolated and perhaps unsure of what to try next and where to go to get support for themselves in their work. Many of us follow a hunch, an idea, and may not always know why something is effective, but discover that it is. Hopefully you feel encouraged now to keep trying innovative and creative approaches but from a position of more understanding about the reasons behind some of the behaviours you witness, why some approaches will work better than others. I hope you'll have more strategies to try with your pupils, and also more ways to make sure you yourself get more support at work.

- I also hope this book has challenged those who may feel that all troubled and vulnerable children and young people need is to have some consistent discipline and firm boundaries. No doubt that's true, some of the time. But they also need **relationships** first and foremost, and an environment where they feel safe and secure. Hopefully this book has also challenged those who might believe that it's unfair to treat some pupils in any way differently from others. My firm belief and experience is that unless policies for behaviour are applied with some differentiation for individual students' emotional state and experience, troubled students and pupils will simply be confirmed in their belief that the world is an unpredictable and unsafe place, that schools are hostile environments, and that the adults who work there will continue to let them down.

- Academic achievement is important for all.   For children and young people who have experienced trauma and difficulty with attachments and relationships, it's often education that provides a future that can be different from that of their parents.   But it's also vital that they learn the social and emotional skills they need to manage themselves in school and in life.   Collectively, all of us working with troubled or vulnerable students want them to be successful and this often leads to the understandable concern when a child or young person is out of the classroom. Somehow not everyone feels the same concern when a student is *in* the classroom, but isn't learning.   I hope this book has highlighted why we need to be concerned.

- Creating environments where every child can learn in a way and at a pace that they can manage is our constant challenge.   Some of our pupils will first need to learn that they are of value, that people care about them, perhaps learn that they are able to learn and that it is possible to feel safe and secure enough to begin the stressful process of learning - and ultimately enjoying - new skills and knowledge.

- I hope there are very few adults reading this book who have experienced what some of these troubled and vulnerable children have lived through.   When we remember the often underrated virtues of kindness and compassion, when we try walking in our pupils' shoes for a moment and realising what they most need, we will be in a far better position to recognise how we need to be and what we need to teach to help them make the most of their time in school; and learn what really matters.

References

Advocate Health Care (2013)
   ahchealthenews.com/2013/05/21/teen-bullies-more-likely-to-become-adult-criminals-study-says

Bandler, R. & Grindler, A. (1975) *The Structure of Magic Volume 1* Michigan: Science and Behaviour Books

Berne, E. (1964) *Games People Play* New York: Ballantine Books

Bombèr, L.M. (2007) *Inside I'm Hurting: Practical strategies for supporting children with attachment difficulties in schools* London: Worth Publishing

Bombèr, L.M. (2011) *What About Me? Inclusive strategies to support pupils with attachment difficulties make it through the school day* London: Worth Publishing

Bombèr, L.M. (2016) *Attachment Aware School Series: Bridging the gap for troubled pupils Books 1-5* Derbyshire: Worth Publishing

Brandon, M., Bailey, S., Belderson, P. & Larsson, B. (2013) *Neglect and Serious Case Reviews* University of East Anglia nspcc.org.uk/globalassets/documents/research-reports/neglect-serious-case-reviews-report.pdf

BBC (2011) bbc.co.uk/news/magazine-15490760

BBC (2015) bbc.co.uk/news/business-30913960

bps.org.uk/news/mindfulness-can-reduce-stress-school-children

Cairns, K. (Associates) (2016) *Emotion Coaching: Helping Children and Young people to Manage their Own Behaviour* KCA

Centers for Disease Control and Prevention (2015)
   cdc.gov/ncbddd/childdevelopment/positiveparenting/middle.html

Childline Annual Review (2016) nspcc.org.uk/services-and-resources/research-and-resources/2016/childline-annual-review-2015-16-turned-out-someone-did-care/

Child Poverty Action Group (2013) cpag.org.uk/content/impact-poverty

Child Poverty Action Group (2016) cpag.org.uk/child-poverty-facts-and-figures

Child Poverty Action Group cpag.org.uk/content/impact-poverty

Cole, D., Martin, J.M., Peeke, L.A., Seroczynski, A.D., & Fier, J. (1999) *Children's Over and Underestimation of Academic Competence* Wiley on behalf of Society for Research on Child Development quoted on academicroom.com/article/childrens-over-and-underestimation-academic-competence-longitudinal-study-gender-differences-depression-and-anxiety

Community Care (2008) communitycare.co.uk/2012/03/22/more-men-needed-in-social-work-says-role-model/

Department for Education (2014) gov.uk/government/uploads/system/uploads/attachment_data/file/335504/EYFS_framework_from_1_September_2014__with_clarification_note.pdf

Department for Education (2013) gov.uk/government/publications/family-stressors-and-childrens-outcomes

Department for Education (2016) *Looked After Children, Data Collection and Statistical returns: Outcomes for children looked after by LAs* gov.uk/government/uploads/system/uploads/attachment_data/file/556331/SFR41_2016_Text.pdf

Department of Health (2010-2015) gov.uk/government/publications/2010-to-2015-government-policy-obesity-and-healthy-eating/2010-to-2015-government-policy-obesity-and-healthy-eating

Ditch the Label ditchthelabel.org/research-papers/the-annual-bullying-survey-2016

Erikson. E.H. & J.M. (1997) *The Life Cycle Completed: Extended Version* New York: WW Norton

Farrington, D., Losel, F., Ttofi, M.M. & Theodorakis, N. (2009) *School Bullying, Depression and Offending Behaviour Later in Life* National Council for Crime Prevention crim.cam.ac.uk/people/academic_research/maria_ttofi/pub16.pdf

The Free Dictionary (2012) medical-dictionary.thefreedictionary.com/Meditation

Geddes, H. (2006) *Attachment in the Classroom: The links between children's early experience, emotional well-being and performance in school* London: Worth Publishing

Guardian (2008) theguardian.com/education/2008/sep/30/primaryschools.malerolemodels

Guardian (2014) theguardian.com/society/2014/nov/14/35pc-children-teenagers-victims-cyberbullying-fears-grooming-tinder-snapchat

Jones, E., Guman, L. & Platt, L. (2013) *Family Stressors and Children's Outcomes* London: Childhood Well-being Research Centre Department for Education.

Lilienfeld, S., Lynn, S.J., Ruscio, J. & Beyerstein, B.L. (2009) *50 Great Myths of Popular Psychology* Oxford: Wiley-Blackwell

Maslow, A. (2013) *A Theory of Human Motivation* USA: Wilder Publications

McCarthy, B. & Mc Carthy, D. (2005) *Teaching Around the 4mat(r) Cycle* Corwin Press Inc.

Medical Dictionary (2016) medical-dictionary.thefreedictionary.com/

Mental Health Foundation (2016) mentalhealth.org.uk/help-information/mental-health-a-z/A/anger/ Motivation Psychological Review Volume 50

Mental Health Foundation (2016) bemindful.co.uk/

Mindfulness in Schools Project (2016) bbc.co.uk/news/magazine-35688048

mindfulnesstips.com/mindfulness-can-it-be-used-to-improve-learning

NASUWT Survey (2015) reported on bbc.co.uk/news/education-31921457

National Health Service (2013) nhs.uk/Livewell/Bullying/Pages/Bullyingfacts.aspx

National Health Service (2015) nhs.uk/Conditions/stress-anxiety-depression/Pages/children-depressed-signs.aspx

National Health Service (2015) nhs.uk/Conditions/stress-anxiety-depression/Pages/children-depressed-signs.aspx

NSPCC (2016) nspcc.org.uk/preventing-abuse/child-abuse-and-neglect/bullying-and-cyberbullying/bullying-cyberbullying-statistics/

NSPCC (2016) nspcc.org.uk/services-and-resources/research-and-resources/statistics/

NSPCC (2016) nspcc.org.uk/preventing-abuse/child-abuse-and-neglect/neglect/child-neglect-facts-statistics/

Office for National Statistics (2013) ons.gov.uk/peoplepopulationandcommunity/birthsdeathsandmarriages/divorce/bulletins/divorcesinenglandandwales/2013

Oxford English Dictionary (2016) en.oxforddictionaries.com/

Radford, L., Corral, S., Bradley, C., Fisher, H., Bassett, C., Howat, N. & Collishaw, S. (2011)
Child Abuse and Neglect in the UK Today London: NSPCC

Reddish, A. D. *The Mind within the Brain* London: Oxford University Press

Schiffman, E. (1996) Moving into Stillness London: Pocket books

Self Harm UK (2014) selfharm.co.uk/get/facts/self-harm_statistics/

Shakespeare, W. (1974) *The Complete Works of William Shakespeare* New York: Avenal Books Crown Publishers Inc

Sounds-write (2016) sounds-write.co.uk

Van der Kolk, B. (2014) *The Body Keeps the Score: Mind, brain and body in the treatment of trauma*
Kindle Edition: Penguin

Weare, K. (2012) *Evidence for the Impact of Mindfulness on Children and Young People*
The Mindfulness in Schools project, University of Exeter